Man of the House

Man of the House

A Handbook for Building a Shelter That Will Last in a World That Is Falling Apart

C. R. Wiley

Foreword by Leon J. Podles
Afterword by Allan C. Carlson

RESOURCE *Publications* · Eugene, Oregon

MAN OF THE HOUSE
A Handbook for Building a Shelter That Will Last in a World That Is Falling Apart

Resource Publications
An Imprint of Wipf and Stock Publishers
199 W. 8th Ave., Suite 3
Eugene, OR 97401

www.wipfandstock.com

PAPERBACK ISBN: 978-1-5326-1477-4
HARDCOVER ISBN: 978-1-5326-1479-8
EBOOK ISBN: 978-1-5326-1478-1

Manufactured in the U.S.A. MARCH 27, 2017

For young men everywhere

Contents

Foreword

Leon J. Podles

Wisdom ascends to the heavens, but it begins on the earth. Proverbs is full of sound advice from a father to a son, who warns, "Folly is a joy to him who has no sense" (Proverbs 5:21), and folly is what we are taught by the gods of the marketplace. The sexual revolution promised carefree, pregnancy-free sex for everyone all the time. And now anyone can be a man or woman or anything in between; the body God created is irrelevant. Kipling warned, "we were promised the Fuller Life (Which started by loving our neighbour and ended by loving his wife), Till our women had no more children and the men lost reason and faith, And the Gods of the Copybook Headings said: 'The Wages of Sin is Death.'"

Chris Wiley provides practical advice for a man to live up to his role as father. Even the Romans knew how important fatherhood was; the paterfamilias was the foundation of the Roman state. But with Abraham the revelation of the ultimate importance of fatherhood began, and at last Paul proclaimed "the Father, from whom every family (patria) in heaven and earth is named (Ephesians 3:14–15). Without a father, there is no family.

The family is a revelation of God's plan for mankind, and the only one who has a higher claim on our loyalty is God himself. Jesus was not devaluing the family, but implying his claim to divine honors: "He who loves father or mother more than Me is not worthy of Me. And he who loves son or daughter more than Me is not worthy of Me" (Matthew 10:37). Our ultimate loyalty is to him, the incarnate God, but under him to the union of male and female that he established at the beginning and which he restored in its purity and integrity (Matthew 19:4–5).

Paul repeatedly emphasizes the right order of the family, insisting that a well-ordered family is a model for the church: a bishop "must manage his own household (oikos) well, keeping his children submissive and respectful in every way, for if a man does not know how to manage his own household, how can he care for God's church" (1 Timothy 3:4–5).

Wiley helps us see what is necessary to manage a household and its economy well, to provide and protect for a family and to ensure its stability generation after generation. Such households provide a space of freedom, the milieu in which a human and Christian life can be lived, a place of sanity and health in a world that seeks to detach individuals from all other connections and make them dependent on the state for everything, to make them denizens of "the brave new world . . . When all men are paid for existing and no man must pay for his sins." But God is not mocked, and "As surely as Water will wet us, as surely as Fire will burn, The Gods of the Copybook Headings with terror and slaughter return."

Leon J. Podles, father of six, is married to the former Mary Elizabeth Smith, who survived a year at Wellesley with Hillary Clinton. Podles survived Providence College and received his PhD from the University of Virginia in, of all things, Old English and Old Icelandic. He helped found Birthright Charlottesville, was a senior editor at Touchstone, is on the board of BishopAccountability.org and author of Sacrilege: Sexual Abuse in the Catholic Church. He wrote the pioneering The Church Impotent: The Feminization of Christianity and the forthcoming Losing the Better Part: Why Men Are Alienated from Christianity. He is a member of Mount Calvary Church in Baltimore.

Acknowledgements

Marcus Aurelius begins his *Meditations* with tributes to all the people who made him the man he was. As with persons, so with books; there are many people who played a part in the writing of this one.

First, I'm grateful to my good wife and our three children for providing me with the occasion to write it. If they were not in my life, I don't think I would have given the theme of this book any thought.

There have been many people along the way who I've spoken to about the topics in this book. Each conversation has shaped my thought. And even though I could never footnote their contributions, their voices are here along with mine.

But there have been some people who have played a more direct role in the writing of this book. Here is a partial list. I owe a debt to editors who have encouraged me along the way; there is John Zmirak, a man who read my early musings on this subject and who went out of his way to befriend me. He worked with me on an earlier version of it and he has been a great encouragement all along the way. Then there is Winston Elliot III, publisher of *The Imaginative Conservative*. He saw something worthwhile in my thinking on household political economy and actually published some of my early writing on the subject. Jim Kushiner, Leon Podles, and Allan C. Carlson of *Touchstone* provided both feedback and support. Besides these, my agent Keith Korman cheered me on during a period when the successful publication of this book was in doubt. John Willson retired professor of Hillsdale College was another cheerleader as well as a helpful critic. But when it comes to volume of time invested, my weekly conversation partners at the Inkling-like group that meets once a week here in Connecticut at a local pub are owed much beer. They have been subject to my rants, and my rough-drafts, for years. Now maybe I can move on and harangue them about something else for a change.

Introduction

How to Build a Survival Shelter

EXPERTS IN THE FIELD tell us there are three things you must do in order to survive in the wilderness. They even give us some helpful deadlines—dead being more than a figure of speech here. And here they are, in ascending order of urgency: you have three weeks to get food, three days to find water, and three hours to make shelter.

The clock ticks fastest for shelter because of nightfall, predators, and changes in the weather. You get the point; there are a lot of ways to die of exposure. Death by starvation is just tedious; no surprise to it at all. Exposure, though—that comes with the thrill of the unknown about it.

Now, there are two ways to find yourself in the wilderness. The first is by coming to the end of civilization and just leaving it behind, either on purpose or by accident—as when you survive a plane crash in the south Pacific, or something like that. The other way is for civilization to just end.

This book is about building a shelter to survive the second scenario.

Too Big to Fail?

There has been a lot of talk lately about the end of the world. This is something of a paradox since the world has seemingly been getting safer and more stable for a long time. But thanks to this safety and stability, each of us has grown increasingly dependent upon things beyond our control. And many of those things have gotten very big and the people who run them, very remote. And this makes us uneasy.

The phrase, *too big to fail* reveals how dependent we have grown. Say it and bank bailouts come to mind. If we lived at another time we might consider the term a vote of confidence. Today it is just the opposite: it is a rallying cry to do whatever is necessary to prevent failure, even if it means selling your children into debt-slavery by running up the national debt.

Banks aren't the only things we consider too big to fail. We could throw in automobile manufacturers, Social Security, or any other really large institution without which we cannot imagine living. We built these things to shelter us. They shelter us from harm, from the vicissitudes of life, even from high prices. And because of their capaciousness, we enjoy more freedom (of a kind) than ever before. They even shelter us from personal responsibility. I suspect this is a secret reason we can't imagine life without them: they not only shelter us from things beyond our control, they shelter us from our own moral failings.

T.E.O.T.W.A.W.K.I!

Every once in a while something happens to remind you just how bad things could get if the things that are too big to fail were to actually fail: a hurricane washes a city's infrastructure away and people run through the streets looting; a subprime mortgage crisis nearly sends the global economy into a depression; Social Security goes insolvent—oops, jumping ahead on that one. I'll leave the rest to your imagination.

I think you can see that if these things collapse many people will be left exposed and vulnerable.

It is enough to turn you into a "prepper". In case you've not heard of them, preppers are people who are preparing for, *The End Of The World As We Know It!* (or, T.E.O.T.W.A.W.K.I! for short).

You could say this is a handbook on prepping; but if you're familiar with other books on the subject you'll notice this one is different. Whereas other prepping books prepare you for a sudden end, this one is designed to help you survive a long slow one. I am convinced that the world as we know it is like a drunk that just won't hit bottom. When things get bad, it sobers up a little and promises to change its ways—then when things get a little better it's back to binge-drinking again. But there will come a day when we find the old boy comatose and gone for good. If we work at preparing for that day we may find that we are more relieved than saddened by the end.

Generally speaking, prepping has an up side and a down side. On the down side: like every doomsday cult, prepping thrives on bad news. If you want to ruin a prepper's day, just mention that the unemployment rate has gone down. There is something untoward about that.

On the up side, prepping stresses self-reliance. Just take a quick glance at the literature and you'll see everything from tips on cultivating heirloom seeds to how to defend yourself with a box-cutter. If prepping amounts to nothing else, it has helped to revive the yeomanry.

But even self-reliance can have a down side. For many people, when the topic of self-reliance comes up, Henry David Thoreau and his little cabin on Walden Pond come to mind. But a couple of things have always bothered me about Thoreau and his little experiment.

The first thing is that Thoreau borrowed his tools. It isn't so much the borrowing that bothers me. I just wonder if he ever bothered to say thank you. It may not be fair, but Thoreau just doesn't strike me as a grateful person.

Those tools didn't invent themselves, you know. The life they make possible, even a solitary one, is a gift. The saw, the chisel, the hammer—these were developed, and their forms were perfected, by nameless craftsmen over generations. Gratitude is called for. And those tools were not the only things Thoreau borrowed.

The other thing that bothers me about Thoreau is the cabin was too small: it was a one-man cabin. I've often wondered if his self-reliance didn't have a little misanthropy mixed in. If it did, there was a little self-delusion in it too. We can't live without others—at least not for long. Our shelters should be large enough to include other people.

> *The Curmudgeon:*
> *Alone in the Wilderness?*
>
> When it comes to level of difficulty it is hard to beat Dick Proenneke. At the age of fifty-one, Proenneke took his tools and his woodcraft skills and moved to Alaska. Single-handed, he built a cabin in the wilderness and then lived alone in it for the next 30 years. Fortunately for the rest of us, Proenneke documented his experience on film. That film is entitled, *Alone in the Wilderness*. Compared to Proenneke, Thoreau was a sissy. But even Proenneke was never truly alone. He took the traditions of woodcraft and wilderness survival with him.

Archeology as Self-help

This book is about building a survival shelter you can share with other people. While I wrote the book, I didn't invent the structure. I discovered it. I should say I rediscovered it. I think a generous librarian could even classify this little handbook as amateur archeology. The shelter I describe in it was very common once. Its ruins are all around you. Once you have an eye for it, you can see it everywhere.

By studying the ruins, and by reading about it in old books, I have been able recover the principles used to build these shelters. They are not too difficult to understand. When you see how they're put together, I hope you'll feel an urge to build one for yourself. To help you see how this structure is often hiding in plain sight, let's begin with a familiar story.

The Three Little Pigs

You remember the plot. Once upon a time three piggy brothers left to make their fortunes. The first pig built a straw house, the second built one of sticks, and the last made his house with bricks. Then along came a wolf. The wolf blew the first two houses down without a problem, sending pigs one and two running on their chubby little legs to the house of pig number three. The story reaches its climax when the frustrated wolf, huffing and puffing and unable to blow the brick house down, climbs up on the roof in order to get at the juicy pigs through the chimney. The pigs hear him coming, and with marvelous speed they whip up a fire. Then they set an enormous kettle of water on it and down splashes the wolf right into it. On goes the lid and, *voila*—wolf stew!

Everyone agrees the brick house was best, but this story is not about the merits of brick over other building materials. It isn't even about the prudence of pig number three. If you really think about it, you'll see that this is a story about a fourth house—an invisible one—the brotherhood that shelters the pigs in the end.

Nothing More than Metaphor?

Once upon a time nearly everyone lived in a house of this sort. They not only housed people, they housed their work, and their goods. I know what you're thinking, Wait, people still live in houses! But they don't, not most people anyway. For most people a house is just a place to sleep, watch television, and maybe cook a meal. Once upon a time a house was far more.

To the old way of thinking a *house* was more than a physical building. It's bricks and sticks were a metaphor for something immaterial, but still very real. It can shelter us in much the same way that a physical building shelters our bodies. And like those buildings, a real house has an outside that it presents to the world, and an inside that its members enjoy and benefit from. This is a household, and it carries some of the same meaning as *stronghold.*

I can almost hear you say, *Ah, you're talking about a family.* But no—no, I am not. While there is some overlap, the two things are not synonymous. You can be a member of a household without being a member of a family; you can even be a member of a family without belonging to a household. A household can even include more than one family. It can also grow quite large. We're told that the biblical patriarch Abraham was able to muster over 300 fighting men from his household alone (Genesis 14:14). Obviously his house sheltered more than one family.

Home Economics

People in a household shelter each other by working together and protecting each other. It is the working together that makes a household an economy and it is the protection that makes it a polity. We don't think of houses that way any more, largely because the economy has moved out of the house. One thing we can say for modern life is that it has a way of cutting things up. We work downtown, we get our food at the grocery store, we go down the block to learn at school, and we get on a plane to go somewhere and relax. Our lives are divided up among highly specialized institutions. But a household is a general-purpose institution. Before we segregated everything in the interest of efficiency, houses were not only economically productive; they were schools, and nursing homes, and dozens of other things.

This is a book about building an old-fashioned, general purpose shelter—a real house—not a house made out of sticks and bricks. This is a good time to build one too; the conditions haven't been this favorable in a long time.

The Divisions of this Handbook

This book is broken up into four parts. It follows a logical progression. The first section deals with how a household is established and then goes on to describe its basic framework. The second is about the material basis of a household. The third section is likely to prove the most controversial.

It is about household politics. And the final section is dedicated to how a household relates to the larger world.

Finally, allow me to introduce you to four personas I will don on occasion. Each will allow me to step outside of the main flow of thought in order to provide commentary. You've already been introduced to one of them: the *Curmudgeon*. Whenever I feel the need to say something biting, I put on his mask. Then there is the *Philosopher*. Whenever something could use a closer look, I'll turn to him. The *Paterfamilias* is closest to the spirit of the work, but there will be times when a subject should be treated but for some reason it can't be made to fit into the natural progression of the text. That's when he will pull you aside for a moment. And last of all there is the *Craftsman*. He goes into more detail on practical matters than can be justified to *Polyhymnia*, the muse of sacred poetry.

Let's begin.

Part I

The Framework of a Household

Chapter One

Covenants

Digging Up the Past

You can learn a lot about life from the dead. This book is designed to help with that. But in order to learn from them you will probably need to get over what C. S. Lewis called "chronological snobbery."

The chronological snob thinks "new" is a synonym for "better." Today, most people think the past was primarily populated with stupid people and that this is the likely reason that most of them are now dead. For example, it is commonly believed that people in the Middle Ages believed the world is flat. But this just goes to show how stupid modern people can be. Most people in the Middle Ages knew the world is round, and the learned even had a pretty good idea of its circumference. Fortunately, chronological snobbery has a cure: reading old books. If you do that with intelligence—and that means with sympathy and imagination—you'll see that many dead people knew more than you do.

But You Can't Turn Back the Clock!

I know what you're thinking: *You can't turn back the clock!* But that is a moral argument trying to pass itself off as a matter of fact. Now, I am happy to admit that there are many things about our time that I enjoy and don't want to lose—antibiotics, for instance. But technological progress can mask regression in other areas—the lack of respect for old people in our time, for example. Progress is not a conveyor belt powered by time. Why, the world we live in isn't even unprecedented. There is evidence of circularity everywhere. As Mark Twain is reported to have said, "History doesn't repeat itself, but it does rhyme." Here's the premise of this book: If our problems rhyme with problems faced by people in the past, maybe the solutions do too.

Before I get down to work I need to say something about my method. First of all, I cherry-pick. This is not a history book. It is a plan of action. I've selected things that I think are helpful for meeting the challenges we face today, and I've tried to adapt them. The past is a big place and some things from the past should just stay there. Second of all, I'm a Christian minister and the Western tradition is what I know best. You won't find anything about the Aztecs here or mating patterns in Irian Jaya. If you're okay with that, then this book may prove helpful to you.

> *The Philosopher: Mining the Past*
>
> When it comes to looking to the past for help, some assume that to praise the part is to praise the whole. Why should it? You can be selective. Making distinctions is a mark of intelligence. Use judgment, discriminate, sort the wheat from the chaff—the good from the bad.

Sympathizing with the Dead

One of the reasons we don't sympathize with the dead is we take too many things in our world for granted. But if you strip those things away one by one, the world begins to look very different.

Years ago I discovered just how much I took for granted when I found myself in the middle of the Navajo nation with a group of teenagers. Back in those days anything resembling a cell phone was only owned by the very wealthy, and we were one hundred miles from the nearest highway. One of the first things a Navajo elder said to me was, "Don't let your girls out of your sight. One of our boys could ride up on a horse and take one of them off to the mesa. You wouldn't want that." He was right; I didn't want that.

I had come from a world that I had seldom thought about. I had left a kind of bubble, but it was such a large one that I had mistaken it for the world itself. The Navajo nation was outside that bubble and I felt exposed and vulnerable there.

The wilderness today seems benign, even vulnerable. But that wasn't the wilderness our ancestors knew. Today we work to save the wilderness—setting up boundaries to preserve it from the ravages of strip mining, or even worse, strip malls. But the boundaries our ancestors set up were intended to keep the wilderness *away from them*. We have succeeded in walling out the wilderness beyond their wildest flights of fancy.

The shelters we live in now are propped up by the immense power of an industrial civilization. To our way of thinking, the stuff they used to keep the wilderness out seems laughably flimsy. Their methods were made up almost entirely of customs, rituals, and symbols. But those things have proven amazingly durable, so durable we can still see their outlines today.

Blood Covenants

The Middle East is a troubled place; but once upon a time things were even worse. It had rampaging armies and bands of thieves. There was regular famine and drought (which helps to explain the warfare and the highway robbery). It was a hard-scrabble world without convenience stores or even refrigeration. You made your own food there, and it was right outside your tent or your window. And if you wanted to keep it you had to defend it.

The fear those people lived with is impossible to appreciate. How did they reassure each other in a way that was strong enough to still their fears? They needed exceptionally strong bonds. Paradoxically, they got them by cutting covenants.

When a covenant was made it was said to be cut. The Hebrew *karat berith* means "cut a covenant." You may have heard that a covenant is a contract. Well, it is in a way, but by comparison a modern contract is a bloodless thing.

Men were always called to witness the cut. What they cut were one or more animals, usually as many of them as were needed to feed the crowd. (Barbaric, right? Wait, it gets worse.) The animals would be cut in two. Then the halves were laid on the ground side by side—joined only by lines of blood in the sand. Then the parties to the covenant made their promises. One might say, "Before God most high and these witnesses, I will be bound to you. When you call, I will come. Your enemies will be my enemies . . . " and so on and so forth. Then the other man would say something similar. Then they would walk the bloody way, getting the blood on their feet and on the hems of their robes. And as they did so the witnesses would shout their approval. Then a cookout would break out.

What was it all about? Why couldn't they just shake hands like civilized people and be done with it? The reason is these agreements had to have some bite. Here's why. When rumor has it that ten thousand Midianites

The Paterfamilias: A Covenant with God

There is a description of an unusual covenant in Genesis. One of the parties is the Lord of heaven and earth and the other is an old and childless Bedouin named Abram. When we are introduced to him his name seems somewhat tongue-in-cheek. But it also seems pregnant with promise because it is a clue that something unusual is about to happen to him. The reason? The name Abram means *exalted father*.

According to the story, the Lord tells Abram to cut a covenant. After Abram does this, he falls into a trance. Then two objects appear suspended in the air—a burning torch and a smoking pot. Then the Lord makes a marvelous promise to the old Bedouin. He promises to make him the father of a great house. After that the torch and pot then pass between the halves.

It is all very mysterious to readers today—but it wasn't for Abram (not for the reason it is for us, anyway). Abram knew what a covenant was.

are coming your way because a plague of locusts has wiped out their crops, and your neighbor between them and you calls for help, what could possibly keep you from turning the other way and running for your life? A handshake? Perhaps—if you are an exceptionally principled man. No, what you need to steel your nerves at that moment is the threat of blood-vengeance. And that's what the covenant promised. When men walked the bloody way they declared, in effect, "If I fail to keep my promise, you may do to me what we have done to these animals." Keeping the promise was life; breaking the promise was death.

In our cosseted world that seems a bit over the top. But if you spend a few nights in the desert without your cell phone even our world can begin to look a little different.

We tend to look back at those Bedouins with contempt and think that the world they lived in is too small for open-minded people like you and me. But we flatter ourselves. We live in a bubble, an immense bubble that we have confused with the real world. Covenants sheltered those people. True, they lived in smaller shelters than we do, but at least they could still step outside and feel the real world, with all its fearsome power and immensity. Ironically the men of those days were actually larger than we are in many ways. They had to be to survive.

Law and Covenant

We tend to think of laws as indifferent or even cruel. If they serve our interests at all, it is only when we have to take someone to court. We never think of them as things to love, or as a way to love someone. Compliance is all that anyone can or should expect.

The making of laws has been compared to the making of sausage. Scraps of disparate interests are pressed together in an unappetizing process called legislation.

But in a covenant ceremony we see a different way to make a law. Covenant promises legally bind covenanters. The bloody mess is somewhat like the bloody mess that accompanies a birth. And like a birth, it calls for a celebration—a big raucous party—because the law and the covenant serve the people that are bound by them. They make the covenanters stronger and more secure. And there are human faces there at the covenant, smiling at each other over a roasting sacrifice.

The Covenant of Marriage

A marriage is a kind of covenant. In fact, if you've heard the word covenant at all it was likely applied to marriage. In a marriage covenant a husband and his wife promise to give each other shelter. You can hear in it clearly in the traditional vows "for better and for worse," and "'til death do you part." Sometimes the bond is painful to bear. But historically people relied on it for a great deal and they considered its demands reasonable. And the covenant binds the man and wife so completely it changes them and they receive new names. A woman traditionally took her husband's name in order to show that she was bound to him; and a man was given a new title, *husband*—which means *house-bound*—*hus* for *house,* and *bund* for *bound.* And here—in the man's new title—we see how one thing leads to another. Marriage makes shelter; it establishes a household.

We have arrived. This is the foundation of a household. A household is established through binding promises made in the presence of witnesses. It isn't the result of two people moving in with each other. It isn't even a contract written in ink. It is a matter of life and death.

A caveat should be added here; it was common sense once, but isn't so common anymore. In the ancient world covenants were usually imposed from above. They bound sovereigns and subjects. A kingdom, for example, was made up of many households bound to a ruling house. You could say a kingdom was a household of houses. The reason this is important to keep in mind is that the work of sheltering each other is not evenly distributed. The responsibility falls primarily on the sovereign. Subjects are supposed to support and defend the king, of course, but primarily it is his responsibility to defend them. The same thing goes for households, naturally. The husband shelters his wife and their dependents, and they in turn support him. That's why this book is entitled *Man of the House*. (I suppose I have now lost the few remaining gender egalitarians who have stuck with me this long.)

The Curmudgeon: Shacking Up

There are many bad excuses for not getting married, but here is one of the worst: *We can't afford it.*

Everyone knows that two people sharing expenses live more cheaply than two people living separately. What these people mean to say without saying it is: *We can't afford the big wedding we want to have.* There is another possibility, one that's worse and goes unstated: *We want sex without commitment.* So, as the euphemism puts it, they *shack-up*.

What these people want is the benefits of marriage—but they want them on the cheap. And the structure that gets built is cheap; it is as flimsy and unstable as a shack. That's why calling it *shacking-up* is apropos. It seldom occurs to them that they devalue what they have by going cheap. But maybe worst of all, they sleazily assume that love is somehow more authentic when it doesn't have all the legal stuff thrown in. This usually comes out when the guy says (it's always the guy): *Hey man, a marriage license is just a piece of paper; what's the big deal?* Well, if it is *just* a piece of paper, why not humor everyone and get one?

The Real Reason People Don't Get Married Like they Used To

We all know that the bonds of matrimony have gotten pretty loose. In the old days this loosening would have resulted in anarchy, but it hasn't today. Sure, many people are a mess and we can often trace their troubles to a broken home. But the world has not sunk into utter chaos. If it had, we would be in the middle of a massive recovery of the old morality. The reason that things aren't worse than they are is we've found ways to replace many of the practical benefits of the marriage bond.

That's the real reason many young people don't get married as they used to. They just don't feel the need to set up house. They are sheltered already. Some folks are married to their jobs; others are *welfare queens* who are married to the Department of Social Services and collect their food-stamps with all the entitlement of royalty. Then there are the trust-fund babies who have never grown up.

And in an appalling reversal, some people actually think an old-fashioned marriage is downright dangerous. Some women fear domestic violence more than a home invasion and some men fear losing their incomes through divorce. For these women, direct reliance on a particular man for protection seems dangerously retrograde and for these men the idea that a wife could be the first acquisition in a pursuit of riches just seems naïve.

The irony is bitter; once upon a time the security and prosperity of a political order depended so much upon marriage the state reinforced the bond through the law. Today so little is believed to depend upon it the legal process for liquidating a marriage can be purchased over the internet for a nominal fee. But what can be done? Since our household arrangements seem to serve little more than our personal tastes, how can the state justify holding people to account when those tastes change?

The Curmudgeon: Sex in the City

Conservatives are sometimes accused of being obsessed with sex. But this preoccupation actually keeps sex from becoming an obsession. Conservatives know that sexual passions have to be controlled if a traditional household is to function. Sexual probity protects the interests of both husband and wife and it secures the interests of their heirs. Progressives are obsessed with sex too, but they are obsessed with sex for its own sake. If sex outside of marriage is a taboo for conservatives, for progressives it is the highest good.

Shell games with words are popular to play when it comes to rationalization. The old notion of *liberty* has been replaced by something called *liberation*. Liberty depended upon self-reliance, but liberation is cheaper; it's nothing but a license to do as you please. But doing as you please can get expensive. That's why liberated people depend so heavily on government largesse.

Preparing for the End

We've lost the felt need for the marriage covenant because the things we've replaced the household with seem almost invincible. What's marriage when you can depend on the corporate economy and the welfare state to shelter you? But things that seem invulnerable can prove to be surprisingly fragile. And things that seem small and insignificant can prove to be exceptionally resilient. What do you suppose a collapse of the banking system or the political disintegration of the nation state would do to the things we rely upon today? If things ever do fall apart my guess is the old logic of the marriage covenant will suddenly look very attractive and so will the old morality.

The problem is most people wouldn't know where to begin. Where household structures still stand they have grown so frail they can bear almost no weight. This is one good reason why you should start working on your own house now. There is another though, one I like even better because it has nothing to do with the prospect of social collapse. Building your own house is a noble and rewarding task; these days, it may even be heroic.

If you long for a greater measure of control over the things that bear most directly upon you, a house of your own is the only way to go. But you must do your building in a world filled with people who will not understand what you are doing. And the champions of safety in numbers may even question the legitimacy of it. But if the members of your house are truly bound together you will all be better off for it. And you will learn the sweet and the bitter of faithfulness and sacrifice. You will learn the true meaning of love.

Chapter Two

One Flesh

And the two shall become one flesh. You don't hear that much any more, but when you do it's usually written off as poetry. With the low regard for poetry these days, that pretty much relegates it to something fit for a greeting card. It's a metaphor of course, one that points to something that can only be found in the marriage covenant.

Metaphors call for interpretation, but that shouldn't discourage you from looking for truth there. We can judge interpretations; some are better than others. And the old hippie maxim, *You have your truth and I have mine* won't work here. The very metaphor we're looking at is intended to bring people together. That's something relativism just can't do.

> *The Philosopher: Getting Real with Metaphors*
>
> Since building a house is something like writing a poem, something really must be said in defense of poetry. Modern people just don't believe a poem can tell the truth; biology—sure, even sociology on a good day. But a poem? Hardly.
>
> Once, when people looked at the world, they believed they could see invisible things. When gazing intently at something that they could see, they believed they could discern the outlines of something they could not—like seeing the outlines of a body beneath a sheet. To this way of thinking the whole visible world is like a poem. Every tree is a metaphor. And even people are fantastically metaphorical; they are images of God.
>
> A certain type of intellectual has been trying to stamp this out for quite some time. He has largely flattened academia, politics, and law, even popular culture. Religion, that great interpreter of the cosmic poem is holding out, but barely.

The Interpretation of Marriage

Marriage today seems to be whatever you want it to be. I recently read a news report about a woman who "married" a tree. (I'm not sure how that's supposed to work, but I'm pretty sure it isn't a union of flesh.) It seems that

The Philosopher: The Symposium

It is possible to find a reference to one flesh outside the Bible, but with a very different moral. It is in the myth of the androgyny as it is told in Plato's *Symposium*.

While in the Bible the story begins with a human being, in the *Symposium* it starts with a monster—a two-headed, eight-limbed absurdity. According to that tale, the thing is so self-absorbed that it offends the pride of Zeus, who decides that he must slice it in two. Now each half longs for the other. (Anyone who has found himself in the presence of two lovers that just can't keep from pawing each other can sympathize with Zeus.)

By contrast, when the Bible speaks of one flesh it begins with a lonely man. The Lord cuts him open and takes a rib. With the donated rib the Lord forms a woman. Then an application is made, "Therefore a man shall leave his father and his mother and hold fast to his wife, and they shall become one flesh."

The moral of each story seems to be the same: sex is reunion. But in the *Symposium* it seems more like nostalgia—a hankering after an original whole—while in Genesis it is progressive, an advance to something new. In Plato, sex is antisocial—a turning away from society, while in the Bible it is the genesis of society. In the *Symposium* the cut is a curse, in Genesis it is a blessing.

we've reduced marriage to one of those games that no one can lose because no one is allowed to keep score. But many children who have had the misfortune of being born into a home where people didn't think you could get marriage wrong know by bitter experience that you can. Sadly, when they grow up many of them want nothing to do with the institution. Maybe worse, when they do give it a shot they miss the target even more wildly than their parents did. People need help. But if they are going to get it, they had better learn to see the truth in a metaphor.

We're not very good at that any more. Facts are the only things people believe in these days. If you can't count it, or in some way measure it, it just isn't true. But human beings are not just bundles of facts. Even when you try to reduce people to biochemistry, biochemistry can't tell you why you shouldn't marry a tree. It can tell you that women who prefer trees to men will be childless—and that if all women preferred trees to men, the human race would die out. But that doesn't tell you why this would be a bad thing. To know why it would be a bad thing you need more than facts.

How to See the Truth in a Metaphor

To see metaphorical truth you need the proper viewing angle. I found a ladder that's excellent for helping with that. It is an old one, but very sturdy. I discovered it beneath a pile of discarded things in the tool shed of Western culture. Of course it is a metaphorical ladder. What other sort of ladder would you expect?

So how do we use this metaphorical ladder with this *one flesh* business? We start on the bottom rung, the one closest to the ground. From that standpoint it is relatively easy to see that the metaphor *one flesh* is referring to the sexual union of a man and a woman.

At this level one flesh is as simple as joining parts; anyone who still works with real nuts and bolts knows the difference between male and female parts. But even so, joined parts can still come apart. The fullest embodiment of the metaphor is something more, it is the issue of the union—the body of a child. A child is physically, and undeniably, a union of flesh. It's a fact. A man and a woman each make a contribution. You can't get a child any other way. The sum of it is: *one plus one equals one.*

The Curmudgeon: D.I.N.K.S.

Back when these interlopers first appeared they were given them a name: D.I.N.K.S.—dual income, no kids. In those days you only found them in big cities. Now they're everywhere. Since they've become the new normal, the name has disappeared.

They used to be considered selfish. What they really are is short-sighted. They tend to think that children are the mistake that people make when they fail to plan ahead. The builders of real houses know better. They agree with every culture around the world, through all of history till five minutes or so ago, that children aren't the result of bad planning. They are the plan.

But this is still only the first rung of the ladder, there are more rungs to climb.

To step up to the second rung you must ask, What *should* come next? When you've asked that question you've stepped up to morality.

Modern people prefer psychology to morality; it makes fewer demands. Morals are so unyielding. Why follow rules when feelings are so satisfying? This is why one flesh has lost any concrete point of reference and has come to stand for emotional intimacy.

Surely emotional intimacy is a wonderful thing, but is that solid enough to build a house upon? If divorce rates and the growth of single-motherhood indicate anything—no, probably not. Feelings come and go; sometimes you don't feel like being intimate, or even talking to your mate; sometimes you just feel like walking out. People used to stay together for the kids—but that calls for self-denial, and that doesn't feel good. So, if you want your household to last longer than many do these days one flesh will need to refer to something more than "that lovin' feeling."

Our ancestors knew this—that's why they turned to politics.

Politics Comes Home

My guess is you think that this is just nuts. You probably think politics is divisive—something to avoid in family gatherings, especially at the Thanksgiving table. You may even consider politics immoral, just a way for powerful people to get what they want from the rest of us.

The word *politics* has a fascinating provenance. It comes from the Greek word *polis*, which is usually translated with the English word *city*. (You can see the connection in the name: Minneapolis.) But polis is the source of other important words: *police* for example, and *polite*. Now how could politics (a subject to avoid in polite company) and *polite* have the same root? Because politics and politeness—and even *police*—should all work like glue to hold a community together.

Plato once compared a political community to a *body*. In his *Republic* he noted that it's a single thing, like a body, yet it's made up of parts—again, like a body. Then he mentally divided up a typical body into three parts: the head, the chest, and the stomach. He reminded us that each has its function: a head governs, a chest feels (he was speaking of what we would call the heart), and a stomach consumes. He then carried these over to political bodies: they need heads—rulers who order the community; chests—enforcers who inspire healthy fear; and stomachs—all those regular folks who are just trying to make a living. And just as in a physical body, the parts in a healthy political body must be coordinated and work in harmony. Sure, things in political communities are never so ideal. But that's why we need ideals; they give us things to strive for.

The Apostle Paul said something quite like this. He famously applied the body image to churches, implying that churches are political communities too (First Corinthians 12). And churches also have a head, which is Christ himself. But instead of stopping with the church body, elsewhere he held up a magnifying glass to it and he identified smaller bodies within this larger one. The little bodies are households. And like their larger host, they come with heads. Paul even mixed metaphors in Ephesians 5; taking *one flesh* at one point and blending it with *one body*, to show that they are both really referring to the same thing. A husband and his wife are one flesh because they form the most basic political community, and they reflect Christ and his body, the Church.

Of course Plato knew all about households, but they made him uneasy. He believed they could undermine the unity of his ideal city with nepotism and other forms of corruption. They might even pull it apart, as each household pursued its own interests at the expense of the community. Households are fine for stomach-dwellers, he said, but anyone who aspires to headship in the larger community must renounce his household for the sake of the common good.

Paul disagreed; he believed churches need households. That's because Paul understood fractals.

In mathematics, and in nature, fractals are all around us; for instance, we see fractals in a tree. The structure of the whole tree is mirrored in each branch, and again in the twigs along each branch, and yet again in the structure of each leaf. A household functions within a larger political body in the same way a leaf relates to a tree. We can't have trees without leaves. If a tree were to reject its leaves, you would have a sick tree, and before long a dead one. Likewise, a household is the most basic community of all; and larger communities depend on them in many ways.

The Philosopher: Houses, States, and Loyalty

The household has always had an ambivalent relationship with the state.

States need households because households produce people. But households have a claim on the loyalty of their members and that is a problem for the state.

There have been many attempts to make people more like insects—to eliminate the household and turn the state into one large hive. One of the most important thought experiments along this line is found in Plato's *Republic.*

Addressing this problem of divided loyalty, Socrates proposes a new class of houseless, spouseless rulers known as "Guardians." Because rule is largely mental work according to Socrates, sex differences get downplayed. And because of the threat of monogamy, with the favoritism that goes with it, sex among the Guardians is on rotation. This solves the problem of paternity—the tendency of fathers to favor their children—because no father will know with certainty which child is his. The problem of maternity is a little tougher to deal with, but it is solved by blindfolding women and removing their children from them right after birth. Children are then raised in common—in what looks very much like the daycares and public schools we know today.

The Part, the Whole, and the Role

This works the other way too. The tree provides the pattern of life for the leaf. Since political communities must have heads, households must have them too.

We don't think of households this way today because we tend to think that people belong primarily to themselves. We imagine individuals as self-contained worlds. And in a universe like that, a head of house can only seem like some alien planet, and every attempt to justify his authority just looks like one world attempting to pull other worlds into a tyrannical orbit.

The Paterfamilias: Reports of My Death Have Been Greatly Exaggerated

Traditionally the paterfamilias served as the head of the house. His rule required no defense; he defended everyone else. Today he is an anachronism; only a real knuckle-dragger would say otherwise. According to all the beautiful people, the paterfamilias is dead.

Feminists would like to take credit for killing him. In a way they did kill him, but not in the vigor of youth, as they would have you believe. The old boy was nearly comatose when they slipped the pillow over his face. He had already grown feeble from lack of exercise, and senile from an absence of mental stimulation. He had sunk to this condition largely because his vital functions had been outsourced to other institutions—institutions, ironically, largely built by him. Now, when it comes to pursuing her interests, a young feminist seldom looks to a husband (if she has one), or even a father, instead she looks to her employer or the Department of Social Services.

A particular boss at work may be autocratic—but what is called for is a better person in the job, not a world without bosses. And when the police are brutal, better policemen are called for, not a world without them. Authority is supported in public life because it serves the public interest. When the household recovers its true interests, the paterfamilias will return.

Are we truly self-contained? Or are we designed to belong to something bigger than ourselves? People who build houses assume the latter. Really, individuals are pretty vulnerable. They need shelter. And when a husband and his wife set up house they find shelter there. They build a common life, and in order for it to be common, the husband and his wife must contribute to the whole. Each needs to give up being the center and enter into a common orbit. And for that to happen they must become parts of something bigger than themselves.

Moving On Up

As with so much of life, we find ourselves with something of a paradox. I began with the metaphor, *the two shall become one flesh*—something that seems to imply a loss of individual identity; and I end with another metaphor, a political community as a *body*—something that emphasizes the importance of distinct roles in order for people to work together.

The thing about roles that unbalances people in a world drunk with equality is how roles result in a concentration of authority in the head of the house. Modern people resist this idea in a household, though they accept it with perfect ease when we speak of the workplace. Of course there must be hierarchy at work, that is where we get important things accomplished. The fact that people expect perfect equality in the home is evidence that they really don't think anything productive happens there. One purpose of this book is to show how badly that idea is mistaken.

But let's get to the next step of the ladder because spending too much time on household polity without getting on to what it helps you do will result in too much stress on the wrong thing.

So step lightly, and let's move on to household economics.

Chapter Three

The Economy of Love

I can read your mind, you're thinking: *But what about love? Isn't that what marriage is really all about?* Actually, I've been talking about love all along. It's just that I haven't been discussing it in a way that most people would recognize these days.

I've been looking at love from the outside rather than from the inside. Typically a book on marriage will begin with romantic love and work outward from that. Then, after a long journey, if it ever arrives at all, it will get to legal and polity concerns. If you have a fuller understanding of love though, those are as important to love as romance.

Even so, from the standpoint of my ladder, you could say that I'm working my way up to romantic love. The intimacy of a husband and wife is not at the bottom of the climb; it's near the top. I'm getting closer, and now that I've come to economics you may at last begin to recognize your surroundings.

I know that of all the strange sounding things I have said so far, this may sound the strangest.

The Economics of Giving

Economics has been called the "dismal science." That may be because for most people economics is all about money. But you can have an economy without money. There is barter of course, but I'm not referring to that. At bottom an economy is based on exchange. And when it comes to that you don't need money at all; you don't even need barter. Exchange is all you need.

When it is put this way you can see that the typical old-fashioned grandma is a very wily sort of economist.

You probably consider the thing we call "the economy," with its markets, its currencies, its inventories, and all the rest, to be mind-bogglingly complicated. And it is. But what you can miss is that all this complicated machinery is really an attempt to simplify things. If you have an old-fashioned grandma you know that a gift from her is never a simple little thing, even when it is just a plate of cookies. Grandma expects gratitude for one; and she expects you to remember the gift, for another. But even more, she expects you to remember *her*. She may or may not put these expectations into words, but even if she doesn't you can feel them in your bones. And there's no paying her back and going on your way either; no, sir. If you doubt it, just try it. Walmart, on the other hand, just wants your money. Sure, it likes loyalty, but only because it wants more money. Grandma is not after money; grandma is after *you*.

Money is a fine thing, but it doesn't have feelings. That's what's great about it. Because of its impersonal nature it makes it possible for huge numbers of strangers to work together to accomplish truly amazing things—like building a car or sending a man to the moon. But it also makes it possible to live without grandma—who needs the old girl when you've got all that cash? You can go buy cookies at the store, from perfect strangers who don't expect you to remember them.

The Curmudgeon: Home Economics

There was a time when husbands and wives didn't work for faceless corporations—they worked for each other and with each other. Discussions at the dinner table didn't revolve around whose turn it was to do the dishes, or who should take Junior to daycare. They talked about harvests and markets, pig iron and forges. A wife was invaluable to a farmer or a blacksmith. He couldn't manage without her. That's because the work of keeping house in those days was the same thing as an economic livelihood. People didn't commute to work; work was in the shop downstairs, or in the barn out back.

For the vast majority of human history a household was a productive enterprise. The word *economy* tells the tale. Like every word, it has a history—it is derived from two Greek words: *oikos*, meaning *house*—and *nomos*, meaning *law*. An economy then is household management—but not in the sense we typically mean today. Today that implies cooking and shopping and making the beds and so forth—things either related to consumption or recreation. While budgeting may come into play, it only does so on the consumption side of the ledger. But historically, household spending also included investing in productive enterprises. Houses made things—food, as in the case of farming, or shoes, as in the case of cobbling—and so forth. We still have households that function this way today, but they are the exception, not the rule.

The Philosopher: Where's the Love?

Empedocles was an ancient philosopher who believed that love is what holds the world together. That sounds sweet—but he wasn't talking about group hugs.

He may have been speaking metaphorically—but remember, people in the past didn't necessarily think about metaphors in the same way people do today. Today metaphors are just images we use to better understand unfamiliar things; any resemblance, however useful, is purely coincidental. But many ancient philosophers believed that the content of the mind and the content of the universe were connected. Empedocles thought that the bond that holds a human body together, and the bond that holds a political body together, is at this deep level the same bond. The name he used for the bond is love.

For grandma everything is personal. She wants to narrow the space between you and her, and to a degree even blur the line that marks where she ends and you begin. That's because she loves you. It's flattering but also a little frightening; flattering because you only want the things you love; frightening because grandma is a little like a Venus flytrap. We don't like to think of love that way. Fortunately genuine love comes with a safeguard. For love to really be love there must be something *there* to love. That means that a little distance is essential to the formula. If grandma is healthy she knows this. And even if grandma's idea of what constitutes a little distance is a little smaller than you would like, she doesn't want to consume you.

What we have here are two economies. One is small in scale, but highly complex; the other is huge, but it boils everything down to things that can be measured with money. From here on out, I'm going to call Grandma's economy, *the household economy*, and the other I'm calling *the money economy.*

Something is happened today that is impoverishing us, even as we are growing wealthier than ever: we're cashing in the household economy. More than ever people work outside the home, exchanging love for money. The household economy is broken. Husbands and wives now have separate careers, separate bank accounts, separate names, and in some cases, even separate vacations.

But the household economy is based on giving. It's emotionally rich and densely meaningful because it is an economy of love. The closest thing we have to it is the economy of God.

Christianity is unique for a monotheistic religion in its claim that God is both three and one. According to this doctrine God is three persons, yet is one in essence. The persons are: Father, Son, and Spirit; and each of the persons is the one God.

If God were simply one, and only one, he would be a *noun* and *nothing* but a noun—the Absolute Noun. Christians certainly believe that God is a noun, but they also believe he is a verb. A plurality of persons makes it possible for God to be both a noun and a verb. What's the action that makes God a verb? The persons in the Trinity give themselves to each other eternally. This is why the Apostle John can say *God is love.*

I hope that you already see how this relates to the household economy. A household is a noun, but it is also a verb. As the members of the house give to each other, the household is enriched. And really, the gift they're always giving is the gift of themselves. Remember grandma's cookies? What did they represent if not her? She gave herself to you in those cookies. Now, tell me, what is the only equitable return you can make? Yourself.

The Paterfamilias: Hierarchy in Love

People *can* be equal in one way and *not* in another. This makes no sense to some people; either people are equal or they are not. They think this way because they believe hierarchies must reflect real worth to be justified. If someone is higher up the ladder, he must in some sense really be a better person.

If the Trinity is our model however, it is not only possible to say that everyone in a hierarchy has equal worth, we must. In the Trinity, each of the persons is equally God, yet each has a function within an ordered hierarchy. The Son obeys the Father, but the Father does not take orders from the Son. The Spirit proceeds from the Father and the Son, but the Father and the Son do not proceed from the Spirit. By using the Trinity as a model for understanding human hierarchies, people are free to honor those above them without degrading themselves. And those in authority can honor those beneath them without any loss of authority.

Two Persons, One Flesh, and the Economy of Love

The giving that should exist in households just can't exist in the open market—precisely because the market is too large and too open. Gift-giving economies can only exist in small personal spaces. Paradoxically, it is because gift-exchanges are too open-ended they must be closed in some sense. There is only so much of you to go around and you can't give yourself to everybody. You are not God after all; you just look like him.

Within a household, a man and a woman enjoy a sheltered space that makes it possible for them to fully give themselves to each other. And at the very center of this very private space they disrobe and are joined. (Or as the Bible puts it, they *know* each other.) The husband gives himself to his wife and the wife gives herself to her husband.

The Curmudgeon: The Brave New World of Baby Factories?

So long as states need children, they will need households. At least that has always been the case. But that doesn't mean states wouldn't try an alternative if one were available. In Aldous Huxley's *Brave New World*, children are produced in batches in factories under scientific management, and they are then raised en masse, like bread in industrial ovens. The very concept of motherhood is outlawed in the interest of something called "mental hygiene." To keep brains hygienic, of course, you need to wash them.

A Household is Not a Closed System

If husband and wife are young and healthy, by giving themselves to each other another gift may form—a gift from God—a child. The child comes to occupy the space in between them. In one sense the child separates them, but in another sense he unites them. And in another marvelous paradox, even though their shelter closes them off from the world, in another sense it opens them to it. A household holds the door open to the future.

As households grow so does the giving. Pause and reflect on what children give to a household for a moment. For years they're on the receiving end of things: they receive food, shelter, clothing, education. In the near-term they seem like liabilities—little cash sinks. That's one reason why birthrates plummet in societies that only look to the market to determine the value of things. Of course, what children give to a household is themselves. And in order to see the value in children you must turn a blind eye to the market. (You can't sell them; let's hope it stays that way.) Yet, in the long run children do give back—or should—often in kind when their parents grow old. That's why, if you're wise enough to take the long-view, children make sense in every way—even in a market economy. (More on this later.) But that's not why you have them.

It is through giving that a household prospers. As I've noted, households can get quite large, and additional members can include people beside children. But at first there are just two—a husband and his wife. But first the two must become one. What seems like a reduction is actually a formula for multiplication. Forget the market economy, with its currencies and all that; it isn't truly real, at least not like this is. It is an effervescent thing, rising from the household economy like a mist. People do not come from money; money comes from people. When two become one it leads to all sorts of things—children, of course, but also Sunday dinners and bed-time stories—why it even leads to automobiles, rocket-ships, fields of grain, and soda-pop. This is why the household is the first institution and the most important. From it every other institution proceeds and what is commonly called the economy grows.

Now that we know what we're building when we're building a house, let's turn to the matter of building *your* house.

The Paterfamilias: Salvation in the Love of God

The Triune God makes a perfect circle, but he is not a clique; there is a way in. According to the Christian faith, the Father gives the Son to the world; but from the Son's perspective the Father is actually giving the world to him. (And this makes all the difference in the world.) The Son then gives the world back to the Father. And then the Spirit brings us into it, taking what belongs to the Son and giving it to us and taking what we give to the Son and making it acceptable to the Father through the Son. This is what is called being *born again*. When someone enters the Son of God he becomes a child of God.

This is what theologians call the *Economic Trinity*. As you can see, it is all about giving and receiving. Christians call it grace because it comes to us *gratis*; we don't pay to get in. In fact, someone else has paid for us. That is called *redemption*. But his isn't cheap grace; it is quite costly. When it comes to an economy of love there is no holding back. When you receive the gift of God you become a gift to God.

Part II

Household Economics

Chapter Four

Property

In the last section I said a household is raised in the following order: first comes law, then politics, and then finally, economics. But to understand them properly, we need to take these steps in reverse order. So the chapters in this section are dedicated to home economics; the section after that is concerned with household polity, and in the final section I will deal with law again, among other things. Why the reversal? Because if a household is not an economy, you might as well toss out polity and law; without an economy they're hard to justify.

In the last chapter I said that an economy can be boiled down to exchange. Let's take a closer look at that. What do we exchange? Labor will work—and I'll get to that in the next chapter. Before I get to it though I want to look at things people exchange—things that usually go by the name of *property*.

In his book *Ideas Have Consequences*, Richard Weaver called the right to private property, "the last metaphysical right." What he meant by that is that even though most intellectuals don't believe in absolutes anymore, at least when it comes to their own property, many of them act as if they do have an absolute right to it. Even a Marxist academic will become a dogged advocate of property rights if his college tries to worm out of his tenure contract.

At a practical level, support for property may just come down to wanting to keep your stuff. Not only do we like our stuff, it is one of the few ways we have left to demonstrate worth to our world—worth here understood as cash-value, but also as *moral* worth. Deep down we all think that wealth should reflect intelligence, courage, and the measure of one's contribution to society.

At an even more basic level, we value property because it keeps us going, it gives us a living—especially currency which we can exchange for the necessities of life—food, clothing, shelter, and all that. Having it stolen cuts deep. It's a bit like murder since all the time spent earning wealth has been turned into dead, wasted time.

> *The Philosopher: Metaphysics? You Must be Joking!*
>
> Making fun of philosophers is ancient sport; they're such impractical creatures, babbling on about this and that. And of all the things philosophers talk about, metaphysics seems to be the most impractical of all.
>
> But there is *nothing* with more practical importance than metaphysics. That's because metaphysics is an inquiry into the basic structure of reality. Because once you know that, you can work with reality instead of against it—like sailors who set their sails to the wind.
>
> What about property? Is it real? And can it be rightfully yours? Believing so seems to have some positive effects. When a person thinks something belongs to him, he takes care of it: and if it is the right sort of thing—it can take care of him. But maybe we're all just fooling ourselves. Maybe it is just a useful lie. Well if it is, then thieves are the only people who know the truth. Hopefully you can see where that leads—to some very real negative effects.

Productive Property

Now, property is not a smooth, homogenous thing, like *Velveeta* cheese. There is property, and then there is *productive property*.

What makes some property productive is that it can give you a living. And it can do that without having to sell it. Other forms of property can't. For example, land can support you. Notice that I used the word, *can*? Take that to mean it doesn't have to. What makes the difference between productive property and just plain old property—what I'll call *personal property* from here on out—is what you can do with it. If you work with land well, it can produce. You can grow corn on it for instance, and then you can sell the corn for a profit. You can do other things with land—you can put a golf course on it, or a parking lot. You are only limited by your imagination, the law, and what people are willing to pay for. You can even lease it out and let others make improvements. But you must retain ownership for it to be *your* productive property—because when you sell it the property becomes *someone else's* property.

To work a property productively, you need to work it wisely. If you don't it may actually impoverish you. Again, take land—even if you do nothing with it, it costs you something. (Think taxes.) And if the land is improved—let's say you put a house on it—there is upkeep to think of. This is why many people who come into property that could give them a living end up cashing it in. For one reason or another they lack the wisdom, or the ability, or the desire, to make it productive.

Often non-income-producing assets are mistaken for productive property because of their market value and their liquidity. Precious metals are a good example. Gold is valuable, but unlike land, it can't feed you unless you sell it. I suppose you could lend it out at interest in which case it becomes productive—but then there is the little matter of getting it back again. Many investments are confused with productive property for this reason—stocks, bonds, those sorts of things. These can store equity, and they may even increase in value over time, but the increase can only be realized by selling them off. It is possible to use them productively by using them as collateral in the derivatives markets. (But watch out! You could lose them if you can't live up to the terms of the agreement.) The point is you must do something with these properties or they are not productive. An exception to this is dividend-yielding stock. That's wonderful to have if you can find it—and if you own enough of it to enjoy an income—which usually means owning a whole lot of it. But dividend-yielding stock gives you income because someone else is doing something productive with property.

What about your house? Surely that's productive property, right? I'm sorry to break the news to you, but it probably isn't. (I feel like Jesus breaking the news to the rich young ruler here.)

Likely you've been told your home is an asset—probably by the guy who sold you a loan. Well, it is an asset from his point of view. It is also an asset from the point of view of your municipality. The reason is your home is a source of income to a bank if it has a lien on it, and to your municipality because it is a source of tax revenue.

So, the only reason you could consider your home an asset—productive property in other words—is if it does the same thing for you.

Now, if your house shelters genuine productive activity—a home office for instance, or a real working shop that makes things to sell—then I take it all back. Then your house truly is productive property. In my own case, I have a home office, and my wife teaches piano from home, together we work a large vegetable garden to supplement our diet—yet most of our productive property resides someplace else. I think that's generally the case today.

So what do I prefer when it comes to productive property? I prefer more traditional, hands-on forms of it—I mean really hands on: land, as

The Curmudgeon:
The Goose that Laid the Golden Eggs

People have known about productive property for a long time. Amnesia about it is a recent phenomenon. Even Aesop, the story-telling slave who lived 600 years before Christ, had a fable about it. It's, *The Goose that Laid the Golden Eggs*. Here it is:

> A cottager and his wife had a goose that laid a golden egg every day. They supposed that the goose must contain a great lump of gold on its inside, and in order to get the gold they killed her. Having done so, they found to their surprise that the goose differed in no respect from their other geese. The foolish pair, thus hoping to become rich all at once, deprived themselves of the gain of which they were assured day by day.

The fable is usually taken as a cautionary tale about greed—and surely it is. But it is also about the foolishness of cashing in productive property. The property is the goose. The moral is plain: care for the goose.

I have already mentioned, rental properties, profitable businesses, and even tools, maybe especially tools. I also have intellectual property. You're holding one of those properties in your hands right now—this book. Any of these things can lose value over time. But every one of them can grow in value when handled property. And the value of each is directly tied to how much income it yields. Don't limit yourself to my examples though. Productive property is marvelously various—there are forms it can take that I can't even imagine. Who would have thought a string of ones and zeroes could add up to anything valuable a hundred years ago? And yet, that is what a computer program is, just ones and zeroes! (In a very particular order, I hasten to add.) What this demonstrates is that productive property is the product of the human imagination; it comes from human ingenuity and plain old hard work.

Let me finish this section with a caveat—I have nothing against gold or stock or any other asset. I hope you own a lot of them. But if those are all you own, you probably work for someone else.

Productive Property and Home Economics

Now, what does all this have to do with the economy of love? Productive property gives the household economy something to work on together, something to offer the world in exchange for a living.

We don't think of our households as centers of productive work. That's because the economy has largely moved out of the house. During the Industrial Revolution steady work in factories replaced the home economy, and many people were forced to leave home to make a living. In the process the household was reduced to what we think of today—a haven in a heartless world—a place to sleep and eat and maybe watch television.

But if your house is going to shelter you in good times and bad, you had better bring productive property back home. There are many benefits to doing so. Here are a three of the more important ones.

Roots

In some ways productive property will tie you down—land for instance, you can't move that; and a business is often much the same. It takes years to build up a customer base and unless the business is completely housed on the internet, you're stuck. But being stuck can be a good thing—trees are stuck because they have roots. People benefit from having roots too. They're good for kids, and for old folks too.

Virtue

When you acquire productive property it changes you. You work with it and shape it. Naturally, it reflects you, like any work of art reflects its maker. But it also has a way of shaping and making you. It demands things of you: determination, resilience, honesty, thrift, practical wisdom—those things. The founders of the United States understood this—that's why the franchise was originally restricted to property owners. Productive property is a school of virtue. That doesn't mean property owners are faultless—just that they are more likely to need virtue in the course of daily life if they are going to survive. What is more, productive property places you in a position to be a net contributor to the common good.

In the United States the old term for this is *yeomanry*. Thomas Jefferson in particular is associated with the politics of the yeoman, which is a bit puzzling since he poorly managed his own affairs and ran up a lot of debt. On the down side, yeomanry is largely associated with farming, and while I'm all for family farms, we need a term that can stretch enough to include other forms of productive property—its acquisition, its cultivation and management, and its stewardship for the next generation.

Shelter

Productive property puts you in a better position to care for people than those who don't have it. Sure, things can go wrong with a business you own—but that can also happen when you work for someone else. (The difference between being an owner and being an employee is who gets fired first.) If a property owned by a household provides a good return, not only do children and aged parents find shelter in that house, but others can too—people hired to work the properties for example, and even the poor. So by working productive property, a household can extend hospitality and be a blessing even to people outside of it.

Getting Property

There are probably a million ways to come into productive property. There is a load of books out there—everything from how to buy houses with no money down to purchasing a franchise. The point here is that when you look to acquire productive property you leave behind the world of resumes, guidance counselors, and head-hunters. You enter a big-boy world where there are no guarantees. If you try and fail, well, welcome to the real world. Get up and try again.

To acquire productive property you will need capital and an idea, not necessarily in that order. If you have a *capital idea*, capital may come looking for you. But if you don't have any idea where to begin, start with capital. Make money. Spend less than you make. Let it pile up while you're looking for an idea. Self-discipline, keeping costs down, working hard—it's the stuff our ancestors did without much thought. It will most likely mean working for others for a while. But that's okay. That's where most people start—I'll talk more about transitioning from that to working for yourself in the next chapter.

The Craftsman
Corporations & Productive Property

Productive property in the modern world is largely in the hands of corporations. Large corporations employ thousands of people, the truly monstrous, tens of thousands. All those people working together add up to something very hard to beat.

The term *corporation* comes from the Latin *corpus*, which means *body*. Due to a strange nexus of religious and legal precedents, along with certain economic interests, these hive-like operations are considered legal persons. A household, even though it has a better claim on being a body, is not considered one. What this means from a legal point of view is that a massive corporation has rights, whereas a household does not.

The Main Chance

You must identify your main chance and that means knowing yourself as well as your chances. It isn't necessarily difficult. It may sound like I'm describing what it takes to start a high tech company—but I'm not. In fact, if you end up buying a small trailer park, or become a contractor laying brick, you'll probably be better off than most people in Silicon Valley. This is the path I recommend—the unsexy path. It usually means fewer competitors and higher profits. You may not end up as a billionaire with a yacht, but there's a chance you could become a millionaire with a midsized watercraft.

If this sounds a little vague—and a little scary: good. I can't give you a step-by-step guide to this. If you need more guidance, buy one of those books I mentioned, or find a mentor; that's what mentors are for. Every way to make a living is a world in itself, with its own rules. My main concern is that you make the acquisition of a productive property your goal.

Rules of Thumb

Still, there are some rules that generally apply to everything. They're rules of thumb because they're generally true and people generally have thumbs—meaning, you should be able to apply these rules.

The Philosopher
The Money Virtues

When someone mentions virtue I bet Mother Teresa, or someone like her, comes to mind. That's understandable, but what's surprising is the circuitous route the word took to come to that meaning.

The word comes from the Latin, *virtus*, which means, *manliness*. (It's where we get the word *virile*.) A long time ago, when warriors were in demand, people made lists of things to look for in a man's man—you know, warrior material. The lists included courage—so far so good, we're in territory we recognize—but they also included things like strength, and even cunning.

Virtue in the sense it was originally used meant something along this line: *the ability to get the job done.* So today, when virtue ethicists say things like, the virtue of a knife is seen in the cutting, you can see what they're getting at.

Put this way, we can see that some things we may not have considered particularly virtuous can be in the right context. Take the matter of building wealth. You can think of it as a ladder of virtues needed to attain wealth. At the bottom you have solid reliable things like a good work ethic and honesty. Above those you could put something like thrift. Things look pretty much like we would expect them to look when speaking of virtue. But wait, when it comes to making real money, we see things come into play that are harder to associate with moral uprightness.

For instance, people who really know how to turn a buck have an eye for value. They can see the money before other people can. They also have boldness in their blood—you can't expect to get the money if you're too timid to go for it. What should we call these virtues? If you're not willing to call them moral virtues, how about, money virtues?

I'm talking art here, not science. This isn't a to-do list. It is merely a collection of truisms—almost proverbial. Make of them what you will.

Recognize Value When You See It

By the time the word is out and everyone wants something, it is too late. It doesn't matter what it is. When everyone wants it, it is time to sell, if you're inclined to sell, not time to buy. The time to buy is when no one is buying—which means, naturally, that the crowd is not what you want to follow.

Seeing value when everyone is blind to it takes imagination and guts. Imagination should be obvious—it is the ability to see things that can't be seen with your eyes. But guts? Yes. Fear blinds. While prudence is important—I'll get to it soon—too much prudence *isn't* prudent.

Counter-Balance Risks With Sure Things (or Surer Things)

Good risk-takers are conservative by nature. If that puzzles you, here's another puzzler—the risk-averse lead the riskiest lives of all.

Every day millions of people take what they believe to be the safe route, placing their trust in people who have no personal stake in honoring that trust. We call the first type of person an employee and the second type an employer. Employees tend to believe in safe, secure jobs, with benefits. Employers know that jobs like this do not exist. Employees usually discover this when they've been downsized, or their jobs are outsourced, or they have been replaced by machines.

The difference between security seekers and people who take calculated risks is that the latter know that life is risky and they live with it.

That doesn't mean they jump off bridges on bungee cords for fun. Most of them work really hard at counter-balancing the risks they take with less risky things. For example, T. S. Elliot was a poet—a notoriously risky profession for anyone who enjoys eating. So what did he do to counterbalance that? He kept his day job as a banker. Wait, didn't I just say that working for others is risky? Yes I did—but there are near-term risks and there are long-term ones. In the short-term working for someone else can make sense. But no one becomes a great poet in the long run by working for someone else.

Avoid Competition if You Can

By the time a business idea is commonplace, the opportunity to get in is gone and the race to the bottom on profits has begun. Forget opening a coffee shop or making videogames. Everyone and his sister wants to do those things. Now, maybe you've got an approach no one has ever tried—fine—then you've got no competition. The point is, no competition is the best competition.

Use Leverage Judiciously

People usually think of debt when this subject is raised. True, debt can be used as leverage—and that's risky. But sailing uses a form of leverage. It's risky too, but not in the same way. If the wind is the force that you want to use; the sail is your leverage. Positioning the sail is how you employ leverage and the wind does the rest. Since the wind doesn't always blow, timing is part of the formula.

So leverage is the use of some force or trend to your advantage. Basically when it comes to productive property leverage boils down to two things: identifying the trend and positioning yourself to take best advantage of it.

It's in positioning that debt sometimes proves useful. Usually it is employed with equities, commodities, or real estate. Let's stick to real estate, since that's what I know best. Let's say prices are rising. You can take some cash and use it as leverage to control an asset through a loan, let's say an apartment building worth $100,000. For the sake of simplicity, let's say you use $20,000 to acquire a loan for $80,000. Again, for the sake of simplicity, let's say that the market is crazy with speculation and it jumps twenty percent in one year. Brother, you're golden now. Your building is now worth $120,000. But think about it—your actual return on equity is one-hundred percent. $20,000 has become $40,000. We mustn't forget that there would be taxes to pay, and there would be a cost to the transaction—lawyers, real estate agents, and so on. Still, you have made a fabulous return all things considered.

That's the magic of leverage. But watch out! It works just as powerfully in the opposite direction. If the market goes down twenty percent your $20,000 is wiped out. (But only if you sell the building; if it's providing positive cash flow, why sell?) Now you know why tremendously wealthy people can lose it all overnight.

Scalable Verses Non-Scalable—Either Can Work for You

Scalability is a form of leverage. Essentially it is the ability to reproduce and expand what you do almost indefinitely.

Franchising makes a business scalable. Where I live there's a *Dunkin Donuts* on every corner. There are many reasons for its success, but certainly scalability is one of them. When a person buys a franchise, he receives a business in a box. The whole Dunkin Donuts model, from food and coffee down to the software that manages the financial reporting, is part of the package you buy when you purchase the franchise. It really is a win-win scenario when it comes to productive property—Dunkin Donuts benefits from the work of the franchisee and the franchisee benefits from the work of Dunkin Donuts. Both own productive property—but one owns scalable productive property (the franchiser) and the other does not (the franchisee).

Non-scalability can work to your advantage too. Take a clam shack on the beach. Since the beach is part of the clam shack experience you're pretty limited when it comes to growth. But if you're the first on the beach, and you do a good job, no one else will try to compete with you unless the beach is wildly popular and you can't keep up with demand. In that case, you may want to expand, then again, maybe you won't.

Again, this list is just intended to get you thinking.

> *The Philosopher: Two and a Half Cheers for the Industrial Revolution*
>
> The Industrial Revolution made our lives better in many ways. We live longer and in greater comfort than our ancestors. But we lost things too. Progress is not a smooth process; it proceeds by fits and starts. For every two steps forward, there is a step backward, sometimes two. It is not a denial of the good things we now enjoy to try to retrieve the good things that were left behind.

Technology and the Surprising Return of the Household Economy

The relationship of technology to the household has been a somewhat ambiguous. First of all, technology played a role in the birth of the household. Without the plow there could be no family farm. And most cottage industry—everything from the blacksmithing to weaving—came into being through a technological innovation.

But the relationship between the household and technology changed during the Industrial Revolution. What had helped bring the household into being now was instrumental in taking it apart. Because of the scale of production, and the cost of the technology required, the household was largely pushed aside. Things were centralized—they had to be in the early days. People went into factories, and later office buildings, in order to work with the people and machinery necessary for the economies of scale that justified the expenses of industrial production.

Soon other things began to adopt the industrial model—education and social welfare most importantly. Children were collected into schools, not because they are more conducive to learning, but because it was seen as more efficient to have a large group taught by a single person than to let children receive their instruction at home. The same goes for the care of the elderly—move old people to the nurses and the expensive equipment; it's cheaper that way. But we may at last be getting off the conveyor-belt and returning home. And help is coming from a surprising source.

With advances in computers, communications, and robotics, industry is decentralizing. Some people lament the rise of outsourcing and freelancing but anyone who cares about the recovery of household-centered economics should celebrate these trends. We could be on the verge of the best of all possible worlds—productive households may once again integrate life without losing

The Philosopher: The Proletariat

People who use the word *proletariat* are usually labeled Marxists; this is unfortunate, because of all the words Marxists use, proletariat may be the most useful for conservatives. Marx didn't invent it, its pedigree can be traced all the way back to the Roman census in the days of the Cesars. It means, *someone without property*.

It can even be turned into a verb, as in *proletarianize*. That's the process of divesting people of property, particularly productive property. Catastrophe or simple prodigality could land a person in the proletariat in ancient Rome. But with the Industrial Revolution many otherwise capable people were forced into it. For example, a furniture maker could find himself competing with a factory. While the quality of factory goods was usually lower, their prices were more attractive to buyers. Soon capable furniture makers were out of work. Sometimes these men went to work for the same factories that had put them out of business.

Marx believed that small independent producers were doomed. Their best hope lay in seizing the means of production (i.e. the factory) and establishing a dictatorship of the proletariat. But Marx failed to appreciate how things that belong to everyone end up belonging to no one. What Communists are best known for producing is dependency and soul-crushing bureaucracy and untold loss of life at the hands of the state.

the good things we enjoy through economies of scale. Maybe those things will even get better. Maybe we can have the independence and the rootedness of our ancestors while enjoying air conditioning, antibiotics, and global markets.

For this to happen, technology and household economics will need to coalesce around new forms of productive property. This is already beginning to happen. For example, a woman in my congregation works from a house that was built in 1752. Because she has high speed Internet, she can manage multiple projects for her clients across the United States. Occasionally she has to travel, but she can live anywhere she pleases. And since she loves old homes, she chose a home built in colonial New England.

The new technology not only makes the development of new forms of property possible, it is actually helping to revive old forms. For example, I recently purchased a hand-forged axe from Latvia. It was made in a remote log cabin in the countryside by a blacksmith. How did I learn about him? *YouTube.* I, along with 300,000 other people, watch him forge bearded axe heads and timber framing chisels on his YouTube channel. He now has a waiting list six months long to purchase his work.

Chapter Five

Work

The infamous sign above the gates at Auschwitz reads, *Arbeit Macht Frei*, or "Work Makes You Free." It was a lie.

I debated with myself for some time about the wisdom of comparing working conditions in the corporate economy to Auschwitz. I run the risk of cheapening the sufferings of those who endured the Holocaust. But I couldn't bring myself to completely disavow the comparison because in some small way the promise that working for a corporation will make you free is being made and, whether it is intended to deceive or not, it is false. Here is the truth: if you do not own productive property you work for someone who does. Ownership is freedom and wage earners are not owners. It is just that simple.

Not that working for a corporation is always bad. As I've said, it beats certain alternatives, starvation being the chief among them. You may need to do it for a while; most people do. But the goal really ought to be acquiring productive property of your own. If you don't, you'll be a wage slave your whole life.

In the last chapter I alluded to the illusion that goes by the name, "a safe, secure job, with benefits". Corporate employers made that up—the safe, secure job part to get people into factories and offices, and the benefits part as a way of getting around the wage controls of FDR's *New Deal*. It seemed like a solid thing for a while, but hardly anyone believes in it these days. That's because no one has a secure job, and benefits have evaporated like a morning mist.

No man goes to work so he can be consigned to a cubicle. Usually he chooses to work for a corporation because he thinks it's the best option available. And usually he hopes a little corporate prestige will rub off on him by the association. But the illusion of job security and hand-me-down social status usually lasts only into his thirties. By then, if he still finds himself in the same cubicle—or perhaps a slightly larger one—he begins to feel like his life is wasting away. This makes him miserable, but most of the time he's afraid to strike out on his own—afraid because now he has bills to pay and maybe kids, probably both. And often he has little to show for years of tedium besides a spare tire and a few work associates he's not really sure he can call friends. Worse, he's likely to have seen a few rounds of downsizing, which means he knows in his heart of hearts that he has believed a lie.

The Curmudgeon: Finding Meaning at Work

It seems that everyone wants a meaningful job. Most of these sensitive souls think meaning is like a treasure hidden in a field. If a person buys the wrong field—i.e. takes the wrong job—he'll never find the treasure. This results in the greener-grass syndrome and a decline in job satisfaction. And no matter where you look nobody's happy. According to the *Wall Street Journal* many doctors actually discourage their own children from entering the profession. If doctors have a hard time finding meaning in their work, we have a real problem.

But maybe people have it wrong; maybe meaning isn't something you find at work; maybe meaning is something you take with you to work.

Freeing Yourself from Wage Slavery

Back in the days when real slavery was legal, at times a slave could buy his freedom. To modern ears having to buy your freedom sounds immensely unfair, and surely it was. Why should anyone have to buy something to which he has a natural right? But life isn't always fair and sometimes you just have to deal with injustice as best you can. At least manumission was an option for some people. It still is today for the wage slaves of the corporate economy.

The first step toward manumission today is taken inside your head. You must stop thinking of yourself as an employee. You must begin to work for yourself. I'm not saying you should quit your job, at least not right away. Remember—I said this step is taken in your head. You need a new mindset. Once you think of yourself in this way, you can begin to take steps to make the ideal a reality.

As I am sure you can tell, I am not a big fan of climbing corporate ladders—I'd rather you built one of your own. I hope you can see why: in a world where there are no secure jobs, owning productive property is as close as you can get to real economic security.

Because corporations own the vast majority of the productive property in the modern world, for the foreseeable future the man who wants to build his own house to shelter his own productive property will need to work with corporations in some way. Now, how can you free yourself from your current employer so you can begin acquiring your own productive property?

I have good news! Your corporate employer may be working at this very moment on a way to get you started.

Freelancing

In an attempt to lower costs, some companies have laid off workers and then rehired them, where possible, as self-employed contractors. In an Op Ed for the Los Angeles Times entitled, *America, say goodbye to the era of Big Work*, Sara Horowitz, executive director of the 250,000 member Freelancers Union claimed that in 2014 the number of freelancers in America had grown to 42 million people and that this number is expected to grow by an additional forty percent by 2020. (Even if these numbers are high, for such an exaggeration to be plausible the actual number of freelancers must be very large.) This development makes sense from the perspective of a corporate employer. It eliminates the employer's contribution to the employee's social insurance for one thing (in the United States that includes Social Security and Medicare). It is unlikely that we will ever see legislation to reverse this. When it comes to the labor market, one nation's social insurance benefit is another nation's labor cost advantage. But my guess is that none of this is news to you.

What may be new to you is my optimism. Getting real is always a good thing, even when reality is harsh. It is only after you accept reality that you can change it.

Making a living in this world has always been a struggle. Our ancestors rose to meet the challenge again and again. If they hadn't, we wouldn't be here.

Freelancing isn't a new thing, you know. The moniker is, but the way of making a living is definitely not. Traditionally tradesmen were freelancers, and many still are. Why do you suppose we call them tradesmen? They go from job to job trading their craftsmanship for currency. Of the trades, builders have probably been around longest. At the top of the heap are the general contractors who sell directly to people who want things built. Then there are subcontractors who sell their work to the general contractors. These men (almost always men) can work alone or they can employ others to work for them. There's no end to the list of trades it seems: painters, plumbers, electricians, metal fabricators, roofers, HVAC men, framers, and so on. A man thrust into freelancing involuntarily won't get much sympathy from these guys. A new freelancer may want to sit down with a plumber and learn how things are done. Oh, and I should add there are also many old-fashioned knowledge workers who have been freelancing for time out of mind: lawyers, real estate agents, accountants, and writers—and that's a very partial list.

Time Isn't for Sale, Results Are

Now both an employee and a freelancer have something to sell. The employee sells his time. From the time he arrives at work to the time he leaves for home his time belongs to his employer. In contrast to an employee a freelancer sells results. He has clients as opposed to an employer. What a client purchases is a finished task by a particular date. But a freelancer often has control over how he uses his time to get the job done. The only constraint may be the need to coordinate his work with the work of others if the project is large. That may mean that the work is broken down into a series of deadlines. On a given day if he can get his work done in four hours, the rest of his day belongs to him. Not so the employee. Since employees sell their time there is no incentive to get the work done quickly, nor is there any reason for the employer to let the employee sit around with nothing to do. If he finishes in four hours the employer is still paying for eight (or more). It's in his interest to fill the remaining time with work. Since a freelancer owns his time, he can use the time he has saved to work for another client. For an employee to do something remotely similar he has to "moonlight" by selling any hours he has left at the end of the day. In Horowitz's Op Ed she cites a survey conducted with freelancers in which eighty-nine percent say they prefer freelancing to a traditional corporate job. Owning your time is part of the reason why.

Now let's say you work for a decent employer who at present has no plan to let you go. What then? Sit content? You're a sitting duck if you do—things can change quickly. How about quitting? Unless you have a realistic plan and some capital, I don't advise it. The old saying, discretion is the better part of valor is a good one. So what should you do?

Make Your Employer Work for You

Many employees seem to follow this advice: *Make yourself indispensible, then your employer won't be able to let you go.* Becoming indispensible is a pretty amazing accomplishment. It calls for long-hours and genuine talent. My thought is, if you really have that much energy and ability, why not go into business for yourself? Even so, let's just grant that you really are capable of making yourself indispensible. Would you really be secure?

Perhaps, if your employer is rational. But can you count on that? Petty politics and short-term thinking often prevail in large organizations. Good people, even irreplaceable people, are replaced every day. Sometimes they're fired precisely because they are indispensible. Indispensible people have a way of making little people who want to feel big, feel little, so they have to go. Sure that's stupid, but sometimes stupidity wins.

Here's some different advice: *Turn your job into a trade school.* Learn things; acquire marketable skills. If you truly master a few, you will at least walk out the door someday with things you can use. (These skills should not be tied to some proprietary thing. If they are, then reproducing them elsewhere would be stealing.)

The Philosopher: What's Free Time Good For?

Josef Pieper in *Leisure, the Basis of Culture* pointed out that the Greek word for leisure, *skola*, is the root of the English word *school*. Surprised? That may mean your schooling was missing something.

To the old way of thinking there was no direct road from practical concerns (what you do to put food on the table) and higher pursuits like truth, goodness, and beauty. To appreciate higher things you needed to step away from your daily routine.

To justify this you really needed to believe in another realm, one that transcends the material world we spend our working lives in. If you don't believe in another realm you'll equate leisure, or what we call free time, with the sort of recreation that does nothing more than get you ready to go back to work.

The three great monotheistic traditions (Judaism, Christianity, and Islam) set aside one day in seven for worship—not just for some folks, but for everybody—no excuses. Why? So that people will be forced to tear their eyes away from the ground and look up.

The Sabbath forces people who would otherwise never have gotten around to it, to consider unseen things above. The best use of free time then is to use it for things you would never get to in the course of a normal working day. This is one of the things that distinguishes a human being from an animal or a machine.

The goal is to bring your work home with you—to make the household the center of productive enterprise once again. This can mean bringing the members of your household into the venture at some point (more on that

The Craftsman: Agency

People who get things done have agency. To build and manage a household you'll need a lot of it. Forget the adage, *Jack-of-all-trades, master of none.* While it contains one important truth, it obscures another. General competence is essential if you want to master the most important thing of all—freedom.

Learning a new skill is like learning a new language. And as with language learning, when you've learned one, it is easier to learn another. When it comes to agency you could say there are four language groups. Once you are competent with one language the others in that group are easier to learn. (Unfortunately it does not seem to transfer from group to group though.) Here are the four groups: mechanical skills, organizational skills, people skills, and aesthetics.

Mechanical ability should be obvious—if you're good with your hands, moving from carpentry to auto-repair isn't too difficult. When it comes to organizing, if you can set up a budget you're probably able to set up an organizational flow chart. Likewise, if you can communicate clearly, you're probably able to get people to work together. And last but not least, if you have a sense of beauty everything from the layout of a vegetable garden to presentation an income statement can be made more pleasing.

in the next chapter). But at a minimum it will mean you will need to move in two seemingly opposite directions.

Household Economy and Specialization

Here's something I've got pinned to my wall. It is by one of the grandmasters of science fiction, Robert Heinlein.

> "A human being should be able to change a diaper, plan an invasion, butcher a hog, conn a ship, design a building, write a sonnet, balance accounts, build a wall, set a bone, comfort the dying, take orders, give orders, cooperate, act alone, solve equations, analyze a new problem, pitch manure, program a computer, cook a tasty meal, fight efficiently, die gallantly. Specialization is for insects."

The economies of scale that the modern world has grown accustomed to require people to behave like bees. But are we insects or are we men? Isn't a man most admirable when he is the master of himself and his surroundings? Sure, to make a contribution to a larger whole, you need to make yourself smaller in a way; you need to specialize. But living a human life is something of a specialty too, and for that you need to be a generalist.

A household is a small, general-purpose institution. It can't do everything well, but it can do many things well enough. This makes it an easy target for social engineers. *Think how much more that could be accomplished if people would just hand things over to the experts!* But there is a hidden price to that: your independence. On top of that, the promises of the engineers are often proven false. But by the time we can demonstrate that things actually can be done better at home, we have a whole professional class of people who have a vested interest in keeping their jobs. This, among other things, is why recovery of a household economy is somewhat counter-cultural.

The Curmudgeon: The Professional

In rhetoric there is something known as *the etymological fallacy*. Here's the gist of it: the roots of a word shouldn't hold it down. What really matters is how the word is used today, and if a word is used in a way that is diametrically opposed to its original use, well too bad for original use.

Many beautiful words have been lost in this way. One such word is *professional*. Somewhere along the way the word has come mean *getting paid for your work*. Ridiculous—that's not what being a professional means. Just pause and look at the word a moment. A professional is someone who professes things. He has something to say. That's why a college instructors are called professors and why religious converts are required to make a profession of faith.

Historically there were only three professions: religion, law, and medicine. The clergy were entrusted with doctrines concerning the meaning of the cosmos, the place of the community within it, and the care of souls within both; lawyers were occupied with the rules governing the community and adjudicating disputes between members; and of course, medical professionals were concerned with the physical wellbeing of community members, particularly the young, the old, and the infirmed. And the crazy thing about all of it was this—money was considered a threat to the professions, a source of corruption, and viewed with suspicion. Men of business, in this old way of thinking, were morally suspect because they were motivated by a desire for wealth, not a desire for the good itself.

What happened? How did this whole thing get turned on its head?

Obviously you wanted people of high character in these professions, so how was that managed? By honoring them. Since what they know is priceless (what can you give for your health, or for justice, or for eternal salvation?) putting a price on these things cheapens them. But professionals need to eat like anybody else, so they were often given an honorarium—an amount determined necessary to live honorably.

But this was resented by one group: the rising moneyed-classes of the late medieval world. Since a disproportionate share of the upkeep of the professions fell to them, the resentment had some basis. So a deal was struck—these moneyed people could join the club so long as they behaved themselves. They too would be called professionals.

This was the beginning of the end. Honor was divorced from the common good and was now accorded to people who were paid for what they did. But there has been a backwash—now lawyers advertise themselves on the sides of city buses and healthcare is now an industry. Even the clergy are honored to the degree they can command large fees to speak at motivational seminars.

Since a household is a general-purpose institution; it should not only be a productive economy, it should also be a social welfare agency (caring for the aged, the sick, and the young), and even a school—especially that. (A typical homeschool outperforms the typical public school academically. And usually a homeschool is run by a mom without a degree, in her spare time, using mail order curricula. What does that say for social engineering?)

Specialization Comes Home

Yet, even though it is a general-purpose institution, within any household you will have some specialization. Often the division of labor will fall along traditional lines. Now, I have known many people who find this difficult to accept. These folk have come to equate freedom with a rejection of traditional roles—and of all the things associated with the traditional household economy, traditional sex-roles is the thing they reject most vehemently.

What they tend to miss is that a household economy is not primarily concerned with that freedom to express yourself. It is concerned with economic freedom. And when it comes to that, the practicality of traditional sex roles is almost impossible to deny.

These people also miss out on the simple joys of intergenerational cooperation that can only be known through traditional sex roles. Mothers and daughters can share in common tasks and a grandfather can join in with a grandson in his work. In homes where everyone is doing his best to self-actualize, people are incomprehensible to each other.

> *The Curmudgeon: Sex Roles are Sexy*
>
> You would think that in our sex-crazed world anything proven to increase the frequency of sex as well as sexual satisfaction would be wildly popular. You would be wrong. A proven method for accomplishing both is traditional sex roles. But for some people accepting those is apparently taking sex too far. One important study has shown that when people move away from traditional sex roles, they have less sex—and necessarily, they have fewer kids. Traditional sex roles are sexy.

Household Specialization in the Larger Economy

Even though a household economy requires working competence in a wide range of productive tasks, a household as a whole must specialize if it is to find a place in the larger economy. Before the Industrial Revolution many households farmed, while others raised animals; some got things to market, and others made shoes. (The list goes on and on.) The same will be the case for a productive household today. Some older occupations can even find new life with a little modification. (Family farming is making a comeback because of the demand for organic food and local produce.) But many households today will specialize in things that people in pre-modern households could never have imagined.

As I've already noted, what makes this an auspicious moment for the recovery of household economics is technological change. Ironically, one of the very things that broke up households—the quest for efficiency—is now breaking up the corporate workplace. People are being sent home, some with pink slips, some with laptops, many with both.

The Curmudgeon: Hansen's Law and the Recovery of Traditional Ways

Historian Marcus Lee Hansen called it, "the return of the third generation." For some reason the virtues of parents have a way of skipping over their children only to be recovered by their grandchildren. Certainly we can see that with growing your own food nowadays. Grandma had a big vegetable garden out back, but her daughter believed all the slick advertising in the women's magazines: anything in a brightly colored box had to be better than what you could grow yourself. *Better living through chemistry* was her motto.

But granddaughter has made something of a return. She's not embarrassed by grandma; she even thinks gardening clogs are kind-a-cool.

This isn't limited to gardening. Even thrift is making a come back. But it goes by other names: recycling, sustainable living, re-purposing. While grandpa may not have had the health of the natural environment in view when he found a new use for that old tire, he definitely had his pocket book in view. His grandson does too, but he has put the accent on a different syllable when he does the same thing.

Hedging

To conclude this chapter on work, let's consider how we can hedge the bets we will need to make if we hope to free ourselves from wage-slavery. Financial planners often advise their clients to hedge their investments. We should do the same thing with other things. When it comes to investments, a hedge is something that actually increases in value when another asset loses value. For example, gold is a hedge for savings against inflation. Generally, when fiat currencies lose value, gold increases in value. When it comes to stock, derivatives can increase in value even as an underlying asset loses value.

Hedging can work the same way when it comes to the things we rely upon in our daily lives. When times are good it is easy to take the things we depend upon for granted. But that is precisely the time to prepare. We should set up our hedges then because waiting until we need them may be too late. The following suggestions are not intended to exhaust the possibilities. They're just intended to get you thinking.

Thrift

Thrift has fallen on hard times. The people who run the global economy seem to want the rest of us to live beyond our means so that we will keep businesses busy making stuff we don't need. It's *the carrot at the end of a stick* theory of economic growth. The carrot forever stays beyond reach and we, like manic-depressives, switch back and forth between gleeful spending and anxious working. But the household economy works according to a different logic.

The best way to keep your money is to not spend it. The adage: *The cheapest car you'll ever own is the one you already have* holds true for just about anything you own. Now thrift requires patience. When things break, if you have the means—and that usually means easy credit—you face the temptation of the quick fix. Almost always it is a wasteful one. For me, my trial has been a washing machine. I own a fussy one. The first time I had an issue with it I felt the urge to dump it and buy a new one. I managed to restrain myself though, and believe it or not I actually got the manual out. I then pulled the machine away from the wall and successfully diagnosed the problem. After I located the part that I needed online I ordered it and in a couple of days I had the machine running again. Not only did I save money, I purchased something money can't buy—the satisfaction that comes from fixing something.

If you're going to be thrifty, you're going to have to be a fixer. And the first thing to fix is your frame of mind. You need to renounce the whole *opportunity cost* mantra people use to rationalize manual incompetence. You know how it goes: *If I spend the time to learn how to fix my stuff, that will mean less time for making money at things I'm good at.* Nonsense. In actual fact it will probably mean less time for surfing the Internet. If liberty is your goal, then a measure of thrift will be needed to secure it. Now, am I as thrifty as I could be? Not by a long shot. But I know that if things were to get tighter, I could get tighter too.

Gardening

You've got to eat. You should learn to grow some of your food. A small plot of dirt, sun, water, and seed—and a miracle occurs—food appears. Amending the soil with stuff you'd probably throw away anyway is part of the genius of it. Again, patience, a willingness to learn, and an investment of your time are parts of the formula. Food is the obvious benefit. And if you learn to preserve your produce you may be surprised the degree to which you can feed yourself year-round. This is stuff our ancestors knew and they would be disappointed to learn we have forgotten. But with the rise of interest in local, organic food, there has been a revival of home-based cultivation. There is even an urban farming movement that is making remarkable strides in maximizing yield in small spaces.

There are many benefits to growing your own food. For one thing, you're reminded that we really do depend upon the gracious bounty of the earth. Farmers are generally more pious than the rest of us. Then there is the exercise. And since the tasks involved are relatively simple there are plenty of ways to get the kids involved.

As usual, the champions of efficiency sneer. But since your goal should be lessening your reliance on economic forces beyond your control, let them. Gardening justifies itself. Whenever your vital interests are served, you are not wasting time. Even if the activity is just a hobby, or is performed ritually; the knowledge is valuable just in case—it's a hedge.

Neighborliness

Insurance is great—I've got plenty. But like everything else in our economy it is hard to see a human face behind the product. But insurance is simply mutual aid on a massive scale. The Amish have insurance too—they call it *the Amish*. And there's no middleman. When disaster strikes the Amish come to the aid of the Amish. You could have something similar if you're willing to work at it. It may not have the drama of a barn raising—but it could. And like insurance, you will have to pay in before you have the right to take something out.

A paradox of genuine self-sufficiency is that it is generally sociable. It encourages neighborliness. The insurance industry, sadly, has contributed to the decline of the old fashioned neighbor. When we give ourselves over to a consumer mind-set, we assume that every need should be met in the market. And we can even feel put-upon when we're asked to pitch in and help out in time of need. But people who emphasize self-sufficiency tend to look after each other. They visit the sick to make certain folks are cared for, or help each other out with small projects (and sometimes not so small ones). And it all adds up. To put it crassly, doing things this way saves everyone a lot of money. But it also helps them feel richer in ways that have little to do with money. Of the ways households can hedge against loss—thrift, gardening, and neighborliness—I admit, I'm not so good at this last one. But my wife is—and that's why the household economy is so great. I'm much better at keeping the whole thing running and bringing in the money and my wife is better at looking in on the neighbors and caring for the sick. She relies on me and I rely on her—it is a one-flesh thing—more on this in the next chapter.

Chapter Six

Help

It is hard to find good help nowadays; that has always been the case, but it is getting especially hard to find a particular kind of help. Here is a little fable to show you what I mean. I call it, *Jack, the Giant, and the Indigestible Bean*. It takes a little time to tell, but I think it is worth your time.

> *There were giants in the land in those days, but fewer people than there used to be. Now the giants were the typical sort—lumbering and hungry. But the people were very odd, most anyways. It wasn't uncommon for a giant to reach right into a house and pluck up one of them while he watched television. No one seemed to mind. Sometimes it was even an occasion for tears of joy.*
>
> *Still, a few people managed to keep clear of the giants, and one of those people was named Jack.*
>
> *About this fellow Jack; he loved a farmer's daughter. One day, as he crossed the countryside on his way to her father's farm, he daydreamed of the daughter and the house they would build together. While he did, he came upon a freshly-ruined house. Flames had consumed its members and all the signs pointed to a giant. When Jack saw that the trail of ruin ran straight away towards the farmer's house, Jack ran after.*
>
> *But he came too late. The giant had come and with the farmer's daughter it had gone.*
>
> *The farmer-father remained and he wore a big smile.*
>
> *"Yep, she's gone," he said, "and she deserved it too. Her grades were good, she's worked hard—we're very proud."*
>
> *"But she's been eaten by a giant!" said Jack.*
>
> *"And a big one too! One of the biggest around, isn't it wonderful?"*

But Jack did not hear the farmer's words. He was already running after the giant. And the giant wasn't hard to track. Wherever it had passed, things were uprooted or broken.

He found it towering behind the crest of a hill. It really was a big one. And it was impeccably dressed. It was lowering the farmer's daughter into its capacious mouth just as Jack ran up. There Jack found himself in a crowd of people, each person shouting up, "Eat me, eat me too!"

"Giant, spit her out!" Jack said. But he wasn't heard over the others.

"Fee, fi, fo, fum!" the giant said, its mouth full of farmer's daughter. "We have one more opening; who'd like the job?"

"Me! Me!" all the people said.

When the giant reached down Jack saw his chance. He shoved a middle-aged man aside and grabbed onto the giant's hand.

"Age discrimination!" the man cried.

"Fo, fum!" the giant said. "This one is a real go-getter. I can use his kind in sales!"

At this point Jack could see that the giant was made up of people. Each digit on its six-fingered hand consisted of human bodies hopelessly twisted together—legs, arms, torsos—all knotted—either heads buried, or eyes blank. Being part of the giant looked painful, and as Jack rose into the air he heard whimpers.

Now that he was high up he could see for miles. Wherever he looked he saw more giants. Some of them fought, rumbling and tumbling, crushing small towns and smashing family farms. Some were so large their heads were in the clouds. Still others were like mountains, with mouths like open volcanoes, other giants tossing things into them. Yet others practiced cannibalism, hunting smaller giants and eating them.

Before Jack could be afraid, he was in the giant's mouth.

He found himself in a waiting room lined with white chairs. The farmer's daughter was there.

"Jack, what are you doing here?"

"I've come to take you away."

"We've already discussed it—I have student loans, I need a job."

"Not here, not with a giant. Everyone is miserable here; can't you hear?"

It was hard to miss—groans came from every direction, the floor, the walls, even the chairs.

That's when the Mouthpiece rose from the floor. She was dressed in a red suit.

"Welcome to Giant Corporation. I'm here to help you find your place," she said.

"Thanks, I'm ready to get started," said the farmer's daughter.

"Stop!" said Jack. "I thought we had a future together, we talked about building a house."

"Jack, be practical."

"You don't have to choose between a house and Giant Corporation," said the Mouthpiece. "If you want to buy a little home our credit union can give you a loan."

"You see, we don't have to choose, we can have it all," said the farmer's daughter.

"That's not what I mean," said Jack. "Let's get out of here—this is no place to spend your life."

"But how can we live if I don't work?"

"That's it—giants take your life, and when you are all used up they just throw you away."

"But you're forgetting advancement and recognition," said the Mouthpiece. "There are many opportunities in Giant Corporation."

Until this moment Jack had ignored the Mouthpiece. But this made him angry.

"Recognition? From whom? People she doesn't even like? Advancement? What's that supposed to mean when nothing you work on is your own? Besides, a wife's place is with her husband."

"Jack, please—you're embarrassing me; we aren't even married yet."

A clicking came from the Mouthpiece. Her head was turning and another face appeared. This one had eyes of flame, her hair stood on end, and her voice sounded like a raven's.

A finger of accusation rose.

"Patriarchy! Oppression! Rape! Shame! Shame!"

Jack began to tremble, but not with fear.

"Hell no!" he said with so much force the Mouthpiece stepped back. "You are the oppressor! And you are a thief! You steal people from their homes!" Then Jack took her finger and bent it back on itself.

"Shame on you . . . ," Jack said.

There was no cry of pain from the Mouthpiece, just more clicking as the head turned again. A new face appeared. This one was made of metal and had holes where eyes should be.

"Business is business," it said. "Nothing personal, but we're going to have to let you go. Please leave by the nearest exit."

"Glad to, but I'm not leaving without her."

"Jack, I don't know. It's so risky."

"Come," the robot said to the farmer's daughter, "you must be processed." It began pushing her toward a back door.

The room began to move. The ceiling lowered and the floor rose and the chairs revealed themselves to be accountants all in a row. They were chanting, "Crunch the numbers; crunch the numbers."

Jack jumped after the farmer's daughter to pull her away, but instead they were both swept through the door. Then they fell.

Down, down, Jack and the farmer's daughter fell until they landed with a little splash into fluid, ankle-deep. They found themselves at the end of a line. Someone came up carrying a clipboard. Its voice was high and it wore shapeless bag-like clothes.

"Oh my—aren't you a buff fellow?" it said to Jack. "And you, with that shape, no mistaking you for anything but a woman now, is there?" it said to the farmer's daughter. "No, won't do, no need for any of that here."

"What is this place?" Jack said.

"Processing, of course," it said with hands on hips. "Didn't they tell you upstairs?"

"What's the wet-stuff on the floor? It burns my feet," said the farmer's daughter.

"That's what we use to burn away anything that isn't useful to the giant."

Jack looked at people further up in line; they all seemed bleached and limp.

"Will it make us like them?"

"Of course! Oh, I know what you're thinking; don't you worry, you two can still have your fun—after hours, mind." It nudged Jack and sidled up to him. "We don't judge here, you know, how you get your fun is none of the giant's business. Why, I imagine a fellow like you gets lots of attention."

The farmer's daughter took Jack's arm. "We'd like to have children some day."

"Children?" it said taking an officious tone. "That's wonderful, I suppose. Let me make a note of that. I should think a liberated woman would not want to limit herself in that way. You are liberated, aren't you?"

Just then some liquid fell from the ceiling as from a bucket.

"Ow!" the farmer's daughter said, "My whole front is burning!"

Jack felt the burning too, just lower down.

"Oh, everyone says that at first," the thing with the clipboard said. "But soon the burning goes away. From the looks of you that may take a little longer than normal, but don't worry, eventually you won't even remember what those parts are for."

Another deluge fell and the farmer's daughter cried out in pain.

"Quick, hold on to me," Jack said. "I'm getting us out of here!"

The farmer's daughter wrapped herself around him.

"Oooo, you two are a problem. We can't process you this way!" the clipboard thing said. It tried to pull them apart.

Jack reached up and grabbed an appendage that protruded from the wall. Then he saw that it was someone's arm. Again he saw that the giant was nothing but people—all knotted together. He pulled himself up, the farmer's daughter still clinging to him.

"Stop!" the clipboard thing said, feebly trying to hold onto Jack.

Jack kicked it away and then began to climb. He saw the hole in the ceiling and he steered toward it.

Once he passed through it he looked up and saw that he still had a long climb ahead of him.

Fortunately he got some help along the way. People in the walls, those whose heads weren't buried anyway, pushed them along. A few even wanted to come.

"Please take me with you," one face said pitifully. "I don't like it here, I'd do anything to get out."

"If you don't like it, why did you come here in the first place?" said the farmer's daughter.

"When I was young," the face said, "everyone wanted to be part of a giant—it just seemed the thing to do. And I believed what the Mouthpiece said. Now I know it's all lies."

"I can't carry you and her, " Jack said. "Besides, you need to work yourself loose."

"Well, I don't know about that," said the face. "Won't I fall?"

"Maybe, but it's a risk you'll have to take if you ever want to get out."

When the face heard that, it was sorrowful.

Then a rumble came from above.

"Ahem! I seem to have something caught in my throat!" the giant said.

Inside, great spasms welled up from below and Jack and the farmer's daughter were thrown up and out into the light of day.

Still clinging to each other, they fell onto a soft patch of ground.

The giant looked down at what it had spat out.

"An indigestible bean!" it said.

With one of its massive feet it pressed Jack and the farmer's daughter down deep.

The indigestible bean was now hidden in the ground and the giant went on its way.

But the bean put down roots and began to grow, and up sprang a leafy vine. In time it came to shelter Jack and his wife, and even feed them. It would be the joy of their life together and they tended it every day. Why, it even lived on after they died, and over the years it managed to shelter their children and their children's children. And that's about as happy an ending as can be hoped for in this world.

The Chief End of Man

The modern world revolves around the individual—his desires, his purposes, his fulfillment. Immanuel Kant taught us that every person should be an end. We call this ideology *individualism.*

But human beings live in groups, which means we are both means and ends, and in that order. Why, even God is both—but the order is reversed. He is the end, but he is also the means. In Christianity God is the means of salvation: this goes by the name *grace.* Getting back to human beings though, The Westminister Shorter Catechism puts it this way: *What is the chief end of man? To glorify God and enjoy him forever.* The end is to glorify God, which makes us a means. We do get something out of this though, something we can't live without—*joy.* But there is an order—first comes God's glory, then our joy follows. It couldn't work any other way.

I suspect you're wondering what this has to do with Jack and the Farmer's Daughter. Getting to this will require a little back-tracking.

The Individual and the State of Nature

One reason modern people play down sex differences between men and women is because it is believed people shouldn't be subject to the dictates of biology. They should be free to choose to live as they please. (A favorite slogan among people who see things this way is, *Biology isn't destiny!*) While this is an important part of the story, it tends to miss the many ways modern institutions help to make culturally destructive lifestyles seem like no body's business. Procreation for example has been reduced to a lifestyle choice and households are no longer believed to be important because social welfare programs and corporate employers seem to have made them unnecessary. *If you want kids, good for you; but don't impose your values on others.*

One irony to all this hostility to biology is it got its start in part with a myth dreamed up by modern philosophers that went by the name *the state of nature*. According to the myth, individuals prescind from social life, standing above it, free of its obligations, and only entering into it when it pleases them. But it is a wholly unnatural exercise—no one can actually do this. And that's not even considering the moral demands of social life. But there is an older and better account of the means and ends of our biology. You can read it in the Bible.

Getting Back to the Garden

When most folks think about the Garden of Eden, if they think of it at all, they visualize it as some kind of tropical paradise—with lots of sun, sleep, and sensual pleasure. They don't really think of it as a garden, something that needed tending. It is assumed that things just grew, without cultivation—at least not human cultivation. You just opened the mouth and the food dropped in. But that's not what the story says at all. The Bible informs us that it was a place to work, a place where man took what God had made and made something of it. According to the story man was placed in the garden to work it and keep it.

And the first man didn't fall into the garden out of the sky. Like the garden, he is a product of the soil. We're told that his body is formed from the dirt. In fact, in Hebrew the name *Adam* means *soil*. (Even our English word *human* comes from the same root as *humus*—again rooting us in the soil.) So Adam truly was an *earthman*.

To a certain degree, we are still products of the earth. Cultivating the soil then includes cultivating our selves in some sense. We should remember this not only because our food comes from the soil—as those champions of organic produce remind us—or because the health of the soil is the basis for our bodily health along with all other living things—as the environmentalists remind us—we should remember this because our well-being in this world depends on *cultivating ourselves*. This is one reason that we refer to the cultivation of people as *culture*.

So, Adam must work the soil, increase its yield—be fruitful. And that included his own body; his flesh was as much the fruit of the soil and anything else in the garden. This is made explicit; he is told to *Be fruitful and multiply*. But that can't be done alone. He needed help.

The Paterfamilias:
What to Look for In a Wife

What you want is a woman from the 50s—not the 1950s, more like the 1750s—better yet, 150 BC. If the objective is to put the domestic economy back to work, a woman who watches soap operas and wears pearls to the dinner table won't help. What is needful is a *Proverbs* 31 woman.

If you're unfamiliar with it, upon reading it you may come away surprised. First, she is *trustworthy*. This is important because she is entrusted with many responsibilities. She is not a slave, or even a servant, she is a steward, exercising judgment and putting resources to work. She is *industrious*, working with her hands. She is *savvy*, buying a field and putting to good use—in this case, as a vineyard. And she is *generous*, giving to the needy. And by her labors her household is prepared for hardship. She is wise and respected. Her many gifts bring her husband honor in the gates of the city—where the heads of houses gather to judge the affairs of the community. So through her labors her husband's status grows. And she is to be praised by her children and by her husband. It is hard to improve on this. This, my son, is the sort of woman you must get.

It Is Not Good for the Man to Be Alone

Up to this point in the story everything is good. Time and again, each new thing is declared good; but after Adam is made, for the first time we hear the words *not good*. The Lord says, "It is not good that the man should be alone."

Today when people hear this most of the time what they actually hear is: *It is not good for a man to be lonely.* Now emotional companionship is sweet. It is truly a good thing to have someone to share your heartaches and hopes with—but this probably misses the point. Unless the story is taking an unexpected turn, we are still dealing with productivity here. It is not good for the man to be alone because he is not as fruitful as he could be. Without the right kind of help, Adam will not produce in kind. After the comic interlude of a parade of animals in which Adams gives each its name, the Lord finally makes a helper fit for him.

Sex as Cultivation

The helper the Lord gives Adam is a woman, of course. But she isn't dropped from the sky; she also comes from the soil; but through a middleman. A portion of Adam's body is donated for the job. Then, when she is presented to him, he recognizes her. She is his very own body. She is there to help him work the soil. But like him, she is the soil; this is subtle—but those with ears to hear will know that this work must include cultivating *her* body, making her fruitful. There is to be giving and receiving; her body is given to him so that he can give something to her.

One of the things that makes ancient literature so delightful is its political incorrectness. Here we have a euphemism for sex. But this is more than clothing for indecency; it is a revelation. Farmers know fertile soil when they see it, and they know what seed is for. And just as the ground is opened to receive seed, so a wife's body is opened to receive seed. The message to the sons of Adam is this: *You have been given a bag of seed to sow, sow it wisely; tend your soil, mount your plow, plant your seed.*

For all their permissiveness modern people squirm here, thinking the analogy unjust. But it isn't unjust. It is an analogy with all the force of fact. And the livelihood of a husband and wife in the household economy depend just as much upon the fruitfulness of their bodies as it does upon the fruitfulness of their other labors, maybe more. I'll show you what I mean in a moment, but first I must address an objection.

The Curmudgeon:
Gender, Sex, and Technology

The number of genders is growing. A person can now choose from a list of 56 of them on Facebook. However the number of sexes remains mired in the past, stuck at a retrograde two.

Gender is what you make it. Contraceptives separate the pleasures of sex from an unwelcome result. Advances in technology now even make it possible to have a baby without the pleasure of sex. Why, scientists are even working on an artificial womb so you won't have to rent one. Progress!

All this belies a single unwelcome truth: there are just two sexes—something that characterizes all mammals—and sex is for reproduction. Gender-talk is an attempt to make something new out of this—it attempts to mix the unmixable, to deny the undeniable. It is essentially a retreat from the real world into a world of our own making.

Our Bodies, Our Selves?

Few things are more likely to elicit howls of outrage than the assertion that our bodies do not belong exclusively to ourselves. A few years back a book was published entitled *Our Bodies, Our Selves*. It became something of a canonical text for feminism. Although I've not read it, I don't really feel a need to. The title says all that needs to be said, and what it implies is wrong.

The title is based on two assumptions. The first is a woman's body should be accorded the same rights as a man's body, and second, since a man's body belongs exclusively to him, so a woman's body should belong exclusively to her.

But what about a man's body; does he really own it free and clear? Men are made from donated parts. The basic stuff that makes up every body comes from other bodies—a mother's and a father's. Because of that, a man's parents have a claim on him. And once a man is married his wife has a claim. At a minimum—she has a right to have his body *present*. Barring legitimate reasons for a temporary separation, if he is available, a man should be accessible to his wife—actually and physically. Then, if there are children, they also have a claim. So, let's review: his parents have a claim, his wife has a claim, his children have a claim—and even his country has a claim in time of war.

Laying all that aside, when we think of the physical contribution women make to the world *as women*, it is what makes them *different* from men that makes all the difference in the world.

The Curmudgeon: What Is the Cost of a child?

Financial planners inform us that a child is expensive. If you have one, beginning with the bill you'll get from the hospital, then adding food, clothing, shelter, education, and insurance—and let's not forget all those unexpected expenses and hidden costs: trips to the emergency room, piano lessons, and summer camp—pretty soon you're talking real money. According to the United States Department of Agriculture, the total sum in 2013, not including college is: $241,080! That's one child; and that's the average. Depending on where you live, the cost can double.

But the assumption here seems to be that a child is just one purchase among others. With this sort of calculus one could reasonably conclude they're not worth it. If you need something to love—try a dog. Think of the money you'll save! You could get a vacation house in the mountains or maybe even travel. And without a bunch of little philistines running around you might even become a gourmet—goat cheese instead of Mac-n-Cheese. The world will revolve around you at last.

More Help Where that Came From

A Haitian friend once asked me, "Why do white people hate children?" After blinking back my shock I assured him that they don't—at least most of them, anyway. But he pressed his point, "Then why do they work so hard to not have them?" What could I say?

A child today is little more than an expensive accessory—like a handbag or a lapdog. That this could be the case just goes to show how easily the facts of life can be glossed over by otherwise intelligent people. Historically people did not have children simply because they liked having little people around. A child was an investment. And like any investment, there was a pay-in period in the near-term, but in the long run people looked for a return.

In some societies the return began right away—far earlier than most people can reasonably expect today. On a family farm a five-year-old could help with chores. And when it was time to plant or harvest, even little hands made a difference. (Anyone who thinks that farm machinery has changed this should visit a family farm.) Things are different these days for nearly everyone else, that's true. Today, when it comes to teaching a little personal responsibility, parents must resort to *make-work*—usually nonessentials like making a bed or mowing a lawn. But if you own a business you don't need someone to tell you to take your daughter to work. She's probably sick of seeing your work. You've probably even put her to work.

The notion that children should be real contributors to the household economy can strike people as immoral. In an industrial economy, years of education, and a good deal of specialization, are believed to be requisite for meaningfully work. Then the horrors of child labor are dredged up—with photos of dirty-faced boys fresh from the mines or small girls dwarfed by mechanical looms. But the fact that children were once so employed serves my point. Boys went into the mines with their fathers and girls went into the factories with their mothers because in the long history of the household economy children have always worked with their parents. Perhaps these photos really say more about the inhumanity of the Industrial Revolution than about child labor.

Honestly, there's just no getting away from depending on our children. We need them—either our own children or the children of other people—not only to care for us when we can't care for ourselves—but even to keep the things going that we think we can replace children with. Think hard about social insurance—for example, programs like Social Security and Medicare. These were designed to care of the aged, the unemployed, and the disabled. But they can only do so through the contributions of the young, the working, and the abled. For social insurance to remain solvent you need lots and lots of the latter to care for a smaller number of the former.

One of the perceived benefits of social insurance has been the freedom it gives people to pursue economic opportunities wherever they may lead. But paradoxically this is one of the big problems with it. It interposes itself between generations. When we come to think of social insurance as a real source of aid, and not just a conduit for redistributing wealth, then social insurance is a snake that eats its own tail.

But what about the private sector? Things work differently there, right? Well, it all depends on what you mean by private sector. If you mean what I think you mean—mutual funds and all that—well, no. It is pretty much the same story.

The Philosopher:
The Children of Men

P. D. James, the great writer of murder mysteries, surprised her fans once with a book that seemed out of character for her. It was entitled *The Children of Men.* It was about a world without children. Something happens to human fertility and the entire human race goes sterile. The reason is never discovered: Is it a virus? Is it something in the water? Is it radiation from outer space? We are never told. And in a single stroke, the two sources of human confidence about the future are gone: children, and efficacy of science. As a result, a cloud of despair descends upon the world. And the last generation, now grown, stands as a living rebuke—pampered and fawned over, it sinks into savagery, hedonism, and boredom—a fitting coda to a civilization that has lost touch with the future.

The book was not a polemic disguised as a novel. It was a meditation on just what children mean to us. We can't all have children, but even those of us who cannot really do rely in many ways on those who can.

Consider this: when it comes to your assets, would a dramatic decline in the population—or even an increase in the median age of the population—increase their market values or lower them? Once again, we confuse a conduit for a source. People make markets—it is the demand for goods that drives prices up. No demand and prices drop. And you need people—productive people in abundance—for demand to grow. Looks like there is no getting away from it. We need our children as much as they need us, probably more. We need to get rid of the lie that children impoverish us—when the conditions are right—children make you rich. You've seen those bumper stickers—*No Farms, No Food*? Well, I have another: *No Children, No Future.*

More On the Making of Children, Among Other Things

If there is one thing I would really like you to take from this book it is this: *people build institutions for shelter.* But here is another thing: when it comes to institutions, bigger isn't always better. Bigger usually comes with hidden costs.

Double entry bookkeeping can help you discover how assets can become liabilities. The thing double entry helps you see is that every liability is actually an asset from another point of view. Take a mortgage—if you have one it is a liability, right? But how does the bank that issues the mortgage look at it? Where does it go in the bank's books, in the liability column or the asset column? Right, to the bank your liability is their asset. Why do you suppose banks lend money—because they love you? They sell loans—the interest paid is the price of the loan. That's their revenue.

Put crudely, the ideology of individualism has turned your child into a liability. Since children are said to belong only to themselves, you are discouraged from thinking of them as assets. Notice how I put that: children are *said* to belong to themselves. But this hides those who truly benefit from your children. Who are they? Just follow the money. Who are you are paying to care for, clothe, teach, or in some other way look after your kids? Those are the people who have turned your kids into *their* assets. And when it comes time for your children to make a contribution to society—don't be too surprised if you get overlooked.

But this system is coming apart at the seams. For the longest time it has been assumed that the drive to reproduce could be relied upon to keep the population growing—but birth control and economic disincentives have changed all that. Turns out people really would rather have a boat than a baby. It's cheaper. Unless we industrialize the production of children—a la *Brave New World*—we're heading for a demographic cliff.

For people to start having children again in the old fashioned way we need to get children back into the asset column of the household books. I'm sorry, but half-measures like more tax deductions (or even cash for kids, like the Germans are trying) won't do. Parents must be the primary beneficiaries of having children if people are going to have them. The fleecing of households has got to stop.

Part III

Household Polity

Chapter Seven

Justice

With some regret, I recall the day I discovered that I no longer had to do what my mother told me. I was eleven years old—a little young, but I would have realized it eventually. All able-bodied young men do. I can't recall what she demanded, or why I defied her. I just remember that she tried to slap me across the face. I ducked. She hit the wall. Then she fled in tears. I didn't cry; and I didn't feel any sorrow. In fact, I smiled.

I stopped smiling when my father got home. He wasn't a large man, and he wasn't a good father either. But that day he did something all good fathers do in a situation like this. He restored order, at least for a time.

On that particular day justice triumphed: might served right.

This is strong medicine, and for those grown weak by a steady diet of egalitarianism, it is probably too strong. Many people feel that a family should be ordered by love, or not at all. And, because honest displays of strength in the service of right are no longer tolerated, people must resort to forms of psychological manipulation—that, or bribery—to try to establish order.

There is another sort of person that thinks that a family ought to be governed by reason, or not at all. But good reasoning is hard work, and it takes a lot of maturity. It calls for humility too, especially a willingness to stand corrected when found in the wrong. Even so, reason isn't all it is made out to be.

You may have witnessed the following scene: a small child has a tantrum, and highly educated mommy or daddy—sometimes both at the same time—get down on their knees and try to reason with the little tyrant. While this is great for expanding a child's vocabulary, when it comes to moral development (or just household order), it can actually be counter-productive. Sometimes the result is an insufferably precocious child who does not respect authority. I once witnessed a mother trying to reason this way with her tantrum-throwing child and in response he started spanking *her*.

When it comes to governing a household, while love and reason are certainly important, what you really need more than anything else is justice. And while love and reason make wonderful counselors, justice depends on something else: *respect*. The good news is that love and reason are right at home in a justly governed household, but without justice, neither love nor reason can remain in a home for very long.

What does household justice look like? Most of us have a sense for it even as children. You can even hear appeals to it on the playground: *Hey, no fair!* Describing it, though—that's going to take some time.

Author! Author!

Rather than jump right in, let's ease ourselves into the subject as if it were a hot bath. Coming at it from the tail end, let's look at what you need to execute justice—namely, authority.

You may think that's an even hotter topic. Authority gets a lot of bad press. That's understandable since there is plenty of historical abuse to document. Furthermore, the very notion that someone could not only have the power to tell us what to do, but even the right to do so, seems *ipso facto* unfair. For these reasons (and more) we have a bumper sticker that tells us to *Question Authority*.

But let's look at authority closely for a moment. When you examine the word do you see anything unexpected? Here's a hint: drop the last three letters. Now what do you have? *Author*.

Authority is born when you bring something new into the world. Here's a thought: have you ever wondered why God is in charge? He's the Author, that's why—the creator of all things. And this holds true for human beings as well. The founder of a business, the founder of a school of thought, the founders of a country—as in the Founding Fathers—these people possess authority because they are authors.

People seldom question the value of authorship. Authors give life to their ideas by writing them down. Once they do that you can enter into their minds and participate in them in some sense. Sure, some authors are terrible; but even a bad author is the god of the world he has made. You may not want to live in his world, but unless his book is assigned reading, you can leave any time you'd like.

> *The Curmudgeon—*
> *The Authoritarian Personality*
>
> Right after World War II the quest was on to identify the sources of fascism. One line of inquiry looked for its origin in personality traits that were believed to predispose a person to fascist politics. So, a group of left-leaning psychologists and social scientists from Berkeley, California, published a book entitled, *The Authoritarian Personality*. The gist of their argument was this: a punitive and harsh parenting style produces a paradoxical effect—a deep, suppressed resentment towards parents along with a tendency to idolize authority figures.
>
> Their work has been largely debunked, but as is often the way of things in the world, the mark it has left seems indelible. The suspicion is that whenever people express concern with upholding authority it is an indicator of psychosis. The need for authority is believed to arise from bad parenting rather than the practical challenges of getting people to work together for common goals.

Roles

Things get complicated when what you make involves people. By introducing people to your creation you have more than characters in a story, or even readers. You have participants. People aren't robots—even when they are your kids. And precisely because they are not, you need to do something to help them work together. This is where roles come in.

Here is an example of what I mean. Take the theater. A playwright relies on people performing their roles. There are roles in the performance, obviously, but there are also roles in staging the performance. Take a musical such as *The Sound of Music*; actors have roles, but being an *actor* is also a role. So is being a set designer, or a make-up artist, or orchestra conductor, or even a playwright. These roles are nearly as scripted as the ones in the musical itself. Without someone playing the role of director, for instance, you're unlikely to successfully stage *The Sound of Music*, no matter how much the people involved really love the story.

Sometimes it is objected that roles are stifling, that they don't leave room for self-expression. Let's think about that. A true baseball fan will tell you that no one played centerfield like Willie Mays. Playing center field is an art—but it isn't free of form. Its *forms* are the very means by which the player expresses himself—they make it possible for him to *perform*. If a ball is hit to centerfield and the fielder is daydreaming and a catchable ball lands for a hit, we'd say: *He's not playing centerfield, he's doing his own thing out there.* What made Willie Mays great was the way he performed as a centerfielder. It was through his performance that he expressed himself. Think of his most famous play, "The Catch" at the Polo Grounds: there was the blind run, the over-the-shoulder snag, the pirouette and throw, the hat flying off. To this day when Willie Mays is mentioned, so is The Catch.

When we return from a ballgame we enter another field with assigned roles: a household. It is *through* those roles that we reveal ourselves to others. As with baseball, or the theater, some roles are essential—you just can't have a household without them. But there is something more to consider.

Craftsmanship

Building a house of the kind I am describing is like writing a book, or staging a play, or even managing a baseball team. But it is also like building a real, physical house.

A good builder knows his materials. He knows what they're good for and he puts their strengths to good use even as he hides their flaws. So when it comes to roles, a little flexibility may be called for.

Building a household is more like building a cob house with traditional hand-tools than it is like building a modern stick-house. Today house building is standardized to a degree that could not have been imagined years ago. Industrial sawmills take trees, and as far as possible, remove all their idiosyncrasies. Mammoth blades cut away bark and sapwood, branches and twigs, to get down to the clear grain at the heart of a tree. Then the wood is cut into standardized sizes—two by fours and so forth. These then are used to form the skeleton of most modern homes. All the chips, waste, and even the sawdust is used to make sheet goods: plywood, oriented strand board, and various grades of fiberboard. Then these are used for the surfaces—sheathing roofs, floors, and exterior walls. The standardization of building materials makes home building a much more efficient process than it used to be.

But with all that standardization we've lost something. All the personality you could build into an old structure is gone. In the old days, when you couldn't run to the big box store, you were forced to make do. You had to hand-hew your timbers. And if timber was scarce, instead of tossing out that twisted beam or gnarled branch, you found uses for them. And in the process the things we'd consider junk today gave those old homes their charm. Branches became trusses, a knotty board became a cutting surface in the kitchen, an odd timber became a mantle. And all of this called for listening to your materials to do them justice, but also to judge their best use.

In a justly ordered house there are roles to assign; but we should also exercise wisdom when working with people and their idiosyncrasies.

Functional Authority

Returning to the example of a baseball team, unless there is a game to win the players have no compelling reason to listen to the manager. A manager can stress his title as much as he likes, but unless there are genuine stakes, even the most deferential player will shrug and yawn. One reason there is a crisis of authority in many households is that everyone knows that there is nothing to lose, because nothing is at stake. (Just what is the head of the house in charge of, the television remote control?) Roles that once possessed authority are now as empty as the titles of European aristocracy. Although some fathers fall back on their superior size and strength to inspire fear, if chest beating serves no higher purpose than shoring up one's ego, a man is a living anachronism—a figurehead and a bully.

The best way to reinvest household headship with authority is by giving households something worthwhile to do. That's why this book begins with household economics rather than with job descriptions and flow charts. First comes the task, then the roles follow naturally.

> *The Paterfamilias—*
> *A House Divided Cannot Stand*
>
> It was Jesus who said: *A house divided cannot stand* (Mark 3:25). His use is interesting—he's defending himself against the charge that he is using Satan's power to cast out Satan's servants. The implication he draws is that even Hell is an ordered house. By the way, Abraham Lincoln used the image too—drawing upon it for the cause of the Union against the Confederacy.
>
> But the principle is the main thing—authority must be undivided if a household is to remain undivided.

Interest

So how do you get the members of your household to buy into this, not just in the short-term, but for a lifetime? To keep people with you, you need to give them an abiding interest.

There is an instructive tale in the Bible addressing this very problem. While we can admire King Solomon's wisdom, at least early on, we can't say much for his son. Something was lacking.

A royal family is a ruling house. When Solomon's son Rehoboam ascended to the throne he immediately did something stupid. Instead of following the direction of his father's counselors when they advised him to lower the punishingly high taxes his father had levied, he called in his old college buddies and asked them for their input. They told him he'd look soft if he did what the old men said—instead they advised him to raise taxes in order to show who was boss. And that's what he did. What do you suppose happened then?

Let me provide a little background. Solomon's kingdom had been a confederation of tribes—somewhat like the states of the United States. The royal house had been established by Rehoboam's grandfather, David. David had been the son of a man named Jesse. And they were from the tribe of Judah, the largest and southernmost of the tribes. (This helps you understand what comes next.) When Rehoboam raised taxes, Jeroboam, a leader from the north, persuaded the northern tribes to unite under him and break away. Here's the goodbye note he sent to Rehoboam, "What portion have we in David? We have no inheritance in the son of Jesse. Each of you to your tents, O Israel! Look to your own house, David" (Second Chronicles 10:16).

And so a house for houses broke up that day due to a conflict of interest. There was no portion and no inheritance for the northern tribes in David (Rehoboam's grandfather). This may remind you of an episode in American history—something about taxation and representation. The lesson here is pretty straightforward—common life means commonwealth. The lesson carries over to any form of government; authority rests in part on the just distribution of its goods—even within a household. It is the goods held in common that provide a common interest. But the goods must be portioned out periodically, and each should get his fair share. And this brings me to . . .

Equity

Giving people an interest comes first, but how do you portion things out? Who should get what, and how much? It is hard to improve upon Aristotle's advice here. He said that justice is equity. In common everyday speech that means you should get what you deserve.

Problems arise when trying to determine exactly what people deserve. What do we merit by virtue of simply being human: respect? the right to vote? affordable healthcare? Where does it stop? But even when we do determine a baseline, we still need to address inequities. When some people contribute more than others is it fair to reward everyone equally?

Now when it comes to inequities due to a lack of effort, things are simpler to deal with. But what about things that just don't depend on effort, but instead depend on outcomes? Here's an example. Take a game of tug-o-war. Let's say you have mixed teams with ten people on each team. Now let's say the winning team includes a slight, 100-pound woman as well as a 300-pound offensive lineman. Now let's say there is a cash prize for the winning team. How should you split the prize? Evenly you say? Sure, if the prize is small, say $100. But what if the prize is $100,000? Would it be fair to split it evenly then? Do you suppose the football player would object? Maybe you could force him to accept it; but could you force him to participate in another tug-o-war? Maybe, maybe not. But you see what I'm getting at—too much equality isn't fair; it isn't equitable.

For some people the cognitive dissonance this creates is too great. Something must be sacrificed. Karl Marx is infamous for sacrificing equity for the sake of equality. Here's his formula: *From each according to his ability, to each according to his need.* I hope you see the problem here—if equity is hard to administer, what can be done about need? Who defines that? We're back to where we started. But equity gets its revenge in the law of diminishing returns. If everyone gets the same thing in the end, eventually everyone will make the same contribution. Translation: everyone will only put in as much as the least contributor. Hurrah! We're equal at last!

When any group of people work together, things will need to be sorted out. There is the whole matter of interest—*having your portion*, as Jeroboam put it. But then there is the matter of fairness: what's fair? Someone must judge.

Securing the Commonwealth

For each member of a household to get a fair share, you need to have something for them to share. And that something would be—you guessed it: productive property. Once you have it, you must protect it. Justice not only adjudicates interests, it secures them. A line must be drawn that says: *Stay out unless invited in.*

The naïve believe that fences are for selfish people. While it is true that fences make selfishness possible, they also make generosity possible. To be generous, you must own something; and if you own nothing, you have nothing to give.

The Philosopher—Varieties of Fencing

Fences seem to work best when they're internalized. A code of etiquette is a fence. A well-mannered person simply observes invisible boundaries that surround other people. He knows where he ends and they begin. And if the lines are not obvious, he looks for them. He feels his way along, as in a darkened room—gingerly inching this way and that until he meet resistance. There are rulebooks for this, but the very need for a manual reveals that some people are slow on the uptake or insensitive—probably both. The boorish person assumes a boundless world. He is the proverbial *bull-in-the-china-closet*, or the fool that ventures where angels fear to tread.

There is no law against rudeness, but there are ways to keep rude people out of your affairs. Techniques of social opprobrium are often used for this. Rude people can be ignored, left uninvited, answered curtly—these are a start. There are groups and then there are groups—sometimes boundary keeping is nothing more than snobbery, a sophisticated rudeness—fighting fire with fire.

But when rules *must* be posted, things have gotten formal enough to require a designated authority to enforce them. This is still one step down from codes of law that call for coercive force to maintain.

The Sword

The Apostle Paul tells us that God entrusts governing authorities with a sword (Romans 13:4). Generally we think of punitive justice when this comes up. That's part of the story; criminals should be punished for their crimes. But when a wise hand guides a sword the cutting can *prevent* a crime.

A sword can serve life. I had occasion to ponder this years ago when my children were born. Before the delivery room was opened to men, childbirth was something of a mystery cult—only initiates were granted access. Fathers were consigned to waiting rooms to wait for news along with everybody else. Today fathers are expected to be there for all the pushing, sweating, and blood that accompany birth. This was true for me. I saw each of my children leave the womb and enter the world. And I felt pretty useless the whole time. I shouted the obvious: *Push!* I also held my wife's hand. And I suppose you could say I was an emotional support. But I don't think my wife really needed me there at all. Her mother or her sister would have been more helpful since they could sympathize with her. But I'm happy to have been there all the same.

It was when my children lay there writhing and crying, that I was at last given something important to do. With all the ceremony of a boat christening, I was handed the scissors. The umbilical cord was then presented. And each time I received the scissors, I thought to myself, *this signifies more than you know.*

Before you can adjudicate interests you need to separate people. For the better part of this book I've placed the stress on the things that bind people in a household together. But paradoxically, the growth and prosperity of a household depend upon breaking it up creatively. (Even the psychological health of members requires it.) For each member to have his fair share, people need to know where they end and other people begin. If you don't define this for them, you will have conflict.

This is why the head of the house must separate himself before he can separate other people. He needs some distance to judge. Motherhood usually precludes this. Typically mothers try to keep their children close. And when children are small, this is well and good. But for the welfare of your house, as well as for the children, and even the mother, the head of the house must stand apart, so he can take the scissors—or the sword—and cut away.

A whole book could be written on this: how and when to separate, observing the strengths and weaknesses of each, putting each into the service of the whole, giving each his fair share—all these things call for wisdom. Done well, everyone will see the justice in it. But before I move on, there is something more to say.

There may come a time, when for the welfare of the household, someone must be cut off and his share removed. Cutting someone off is painful, but when it is done, a sharp edge can make it quick. And this should bring you back to where I began. When it comes to household order, *might must serve right*. In the vast majority of households the father is best equipped for the job. That doesn't mean it will be easy for you to do this if ever you must. This is precisely why you should prepare yourself beforehand in case it should come to that. How do you manage that? It calls for something called *gravitas*.

Chapter Eight

Gravitas

Some guys like to keep things light. It keeps them from having to shoulder heavy responsibilities. I'm not saying these guys are completely irresponsible. Some of them are capable of what could be called *generic parenting*. What I mean by that is they're nurturing.

Now, I'm not down on nurture. It is a beautiful thing; I wouldn't be here without it, and neither would you. Nurture draws you in, it tends to narrow distances; it almost absorbs you, like a return to the womb. If you've been traumatized, really hurt in someway, it is exactly what you need. But it isn't the only thing that's needed when it comes to running a household. And frankly, most men can't match the average woman in this regard. It is hard to take a man seriously when he's trying to do something he's just not very well equipped for. If that's you, give up. You'll always be *mommy second-class*—and even though your wife will appreciate the help when it comes to diaper changing, she probably wants a monopoly on mommy-hood.

But guys who just want to keep things light don't have to be nurturing; sometimes they just want to be liked. While mommy second-class is a nurturer, *buddy-dad* just wants to be a friend. To pull that off, he has to level things out a bit. That's because a buddy is a companion, an equal. Aristotle—that no nonsense philosopher—said that equality is a must when it comes to friendship. When buddy-dad befriends his kids he's actually abdicating fatherhood, at least temporarily. It is usually an unconscious decision, and sometimes he comes to regret it, usually when discipline is called for. Often, that's when buddy-dad realizes that no one takes him seriously.

Why You Need to Put On Weight and Keep It On

As with any institution, nurture and friendship are just not enough to keep a household going. Even in the best of circumstances sooner or later you'll need justice. And when it comes to justice, nurture and friendship can actually get in the way. A judge has to separate himself from people and rise above them. Paradoxically, to do that you need to put on weight; you need *gravitas*.

I think you know what I mean. We've all known people that just can't be taken lightly. When one of these people enters a room you feel his presence, your eyes lower and so does your voice.

In the high school I attended we had a vice principal charged with school discipline. Talk about gravitas—he weighed a ton. His name was Shue—Mr. Shue to you and me. No one knew his first name; he probably didn't have one. Or maybe his mother just named him, *Mister*. All I know is that he was universally feared. Even teachers feared him.

Now you may be thinking: *How awful—no one should be feared!* Really? Here is a little anecdote to show you just how wonderful it can be to fear someone. I recall an incident on a school bus at the end of the day. The bus was full and we were waiting to leave behind a long line of buses. Some of the rowdier guys in the back—tough kids, drug-users, you know the sort—were teasing and bullying kids near them. Our fat bus-driver was a lightweight. He squeaked from the front something that might be interpreted to mean, "Please, stop." There was laughter and someone shouted, "Shut up, old man!" Other kids, nerds and such, slid down their seats and prayed for a quick ride home. They had seen this movie before and everyone knew how it ended. Then a voice from the back said, "Cool it! It's Mr. Shue!"

Mr. Shue was walking toward the bus, no hurry, just a man in a dark suit looking in our direction. You could feel the atmosphere change in the bus—the burden of dread oppressing the weak now shifted and began to weigh down the strong. When Mr. Shue stepped onto the bus and ascended the short set of stairs, he was greeted with silence. He looked us over, scanning faces. He didn't say anything, just stood there, projecting authority effortlessly, like a fireman shooting water from a hose. Then he pointed at two boys in the back and beckoned them to follow him. Then he stepped out of the bus and walked away. The boys silently got up and went. We all watched them follow Mr. Shue into the building. If I recall correctly, Mr. Shue never looked back to see if they were coming.

That's gravitas, man. You want it.

What Is Gravitas?

The Paterfamilias—Put Weight On Before You Throw It Around

This maybe the most important among the many paradoxes of gravitas: the more you weigh, the less you need to throw your weight around. Gravitas is something that can be felt at a distance—like the mass of objects in outer space: the larger the object, the greater the gravity.

If a man finds himself in need of gravitas before he has acquired it, the difficulty in getting it goes up to the degree he lacks it. Size matters, people who lack physical size often have to purchase gravitas again and again (usually through conspicuous accomplishment) until their reputations are large enough to make up for a lack of size. Other people are lent it immediately based upon appearance, but those people can lose it quickly if they fail to justify the credit that has been extended to them. Getting that credit back can be nearly impossible once lost. That's because such a person has become ridiculous, like a performing elephant.

Essentially though, gravitas is a state of mind that is reflected in the minds of others. Unless a man first believes he is worthy of respect others will agree with him that he is not.

Antonyms can help you define something as well as synonyms—maybe better. Levity is the opposite of gravitas. Levity is humor; it lightens things up: it seems to make things levitate. When someone says, "lighten up" he's encouraging this. Sometimes things do get too heavy and you really do need to lighten up. That's why medieval courts had jesters; you can do with a little comic relief once in a while. Aristotle even identified *wittiness* as a virtue.

But sometimes things get too light. Our time is characterized by a retreat into irony. Everyone wants to remain aloof, to float away from entangling commitments. We don't want things to stir our emotions too much, or tie us down with unsought obligations.

As you can see in my little anecdote about Mr. Shue, gravitas is for serious people. Serious people take things seriously and they expect you to too.

In case you haven't picked up on it by now, *gravitas* is Latin for *heavy*. It should get you thinking of a related word—*gravity*. When we think of gravity we imagine things falling to the ground, like Newton's apple. When you feel the weight of some responsibility you might find yourself saying you *feel its gravity*. You may even feel like falling to the ground yourself and crying out for mercy. Gravitas was not so much something Mr. Shue possessed as much as a psychological state he produced in people, something akin to dread.

This is what the Romans meant when they spoke of gravitas. They noticed that some men have weight—and they naturally make others feel it. To the Roman way of thinking this is a virtue. It's a virtue because it is useful for certain things. For one thing, it can help you maintain a productive order. For another it can serve justice; they thought justice is unimaginable without it.

I'm afraid this is where egalitarians find themselves in a bit of a bind. Equality actually undermines the very thing that is required to support it. It brings *The Wizard of Oz* to mind. There's a twist, though. In the story the Wizard was an utterly unintimidating little fellow hiding behind an image of great power—but in our case things are reversed: an immensely powerful bureaucratic state hides behind a curtain of egalitarian ideology. The projected image is not a frightening one of power and flame. Instead politicians do their best to look just like everybody else. But don't be fooled. Defy the state and you will feel the full weight of its coercive force. For all their shortcomings, one thing we can say for the Romans is they were honest about power.

Here's something else egalitarians don't like about gravitas: it is easier for men to acquire it than women. Physical strength is a big reason, but not the only one—height helps—as does a deeper voice. (Ever notice how women in positions of authority tend to lower their voices? Of course, no one is permitted to note such things in an egalitarian society.) These aren't enough though. To have real weight, you must be able to bring force to bear.

Think of a continuum, with nurture at one end and gravitas at the other. The more you go toward the one, the further you get from the other. Gravitas weighs on us because we know a man with gravitas is not only willing to cut us off, he has the power to do it. That's what made Mr. Shue so intimidating. Not only did he have a face of stone, he really could cut you off. He could cut you off from freedom, from friends, even from school. No matter how much kids feigned too cool for school, they knew deep down that no one was too cool for Mr. Shue.

This doesn't mean that an authority figure must be completely unfeeling. Gravitas is not the only virtue you will need if you want to be something more than a heavy. But the line separating a good ruler from a tyrant is thinner than most people suppose. Both have gravitas. Gravitas is somewhat like nuclear fission. Fission can light a city, or it can wipe it out. The difference is moral purpose. Or put it this way—gravitas is in itself amoral. In the hands of a bad man it is deadly; but in the hands of a good man it protects life.

The Curmudgeon—Marry a Woman Who Loves Men In General, Not Just One Man In Particular

Some women dislike men. These women are always on the lookout for ways to take men lightly. A woman like this can makes a man's work in a household difficult.

There is another kind of woman, rare in the world today and getting rarer (and by implication more valuable) who loves men in general and depends upon them.

These women do not compete with men or try to replace them, but seek to complement them in both words and deeds. They even take pride in knowing men.

These women are disappearing because of persecution by feminists. At all costs, marry a woman who genuinely loves men. She will support your weight rather than try to strip you of it.

The Paradox of Manliness and Gravitas

When it comes to making a living in this world it is easy to see that individuals living alone don't fare as well people living in groups. When it comes to individuals though, one class of persons is better equipped to go it alone than any of the others. That person is the able-bodied adult male in the prime of life. You don't need to look to mountain men for evidence. You can see this in urban environments. When it comes to people surviving on the street, by my guesstimate men outnumber women 10 to 1. You may write that off as stubbornness or stupidity—no matter, it demonstrates the point: able-bodied adult men are better equipped to go it alone than other people.

A healthy man is simply better fit to go it alone. Generally he's stronger, his skin is thicker, his heart is larger (which keeps him warmer), and usually his eye-to-hand coordination is better. Even his brain is better equipped for the task. Men can build better and faster, plant and harvest more productively, and kill more efficiently and with less remorse than most women. This places a man in a very advantageous position when it comes to dealing with other people. Simply put: *they need him more than he needs them.*

Anyone who has done any haggling knows it is the party that can walk away who has leverage. This is why young men challenge authority more often than other people. It isn't just hormones; many men really *can* just walk away. This is also a reason entrepreneurs are more likely to be young men.

Paradoxically, this is one big reason why men find themselves in positions of authority over time. They're the ones who start the businesses, and when they're successful they don't simply hand things over to someone else because that would be fair. Academics puzzle over the incongruity of academic achievement for women failing to translate into achievement elsewhere in society. But there is only a modest relationship between a good grade-point average and economic success. Students who make their teachers happy do so by excelling in a highly controlled environment. They're neat and prompt and they properly cite their sources, among other things. So long as they stay in school, this works great. But entrepreneurs really don't care about any of those things. Now an entrepreneur may want those things in his employees—but that's why they work for him and not the other way around. Generally PhDs make great administrative assistants.

What does this have to do with gravitas? Boiled down gravitas starts with, "Who needs you?" And unless you can say it and really mean it, you have no gravitas.

That's where it starts, but without something extra you'll just end up living alone in the woods (or on the street). Here are three things you'll need if you want gravitas to work for you.

Tips for Putting On Weight

Self-Mastery

Perhaps the thing that distinguishes a just man from a tyrant more than anything else is self-mastery. Tyrants manage to gain mastery over others without first mastering themselves. When this happens the people a ruler should serve become his slaves. This master/slave arrangement is somewhat misleading though, because the tyrant is also a slave. He is a slave to his appetites. And since he is never free of them, he is never truly free to serve anyone else.

Here's something else to consider: the constitution of your soul will be reflected in the constitution of your house. If that sounds odd it maybe because you have confused documents with constitutions. A constitution is an order, whether it is documented or not. In the same way that scientists attempt to document the natural order, a written constitution is an attempt to document a civic order. But no one thinks that nature is unordered before scientists show up. Likewise, a civic order exists before it is documented. In the United States the founders of our country wanted to preserve certain aspects of their civic order because they believed those things are true in a way that transcends time. (Whether that is true or not is something you can find discussed in other books. I happen to believe they did have many things right.) My concern here is to help you see something that you may not have considered. A constitution is an order—and like any order, it can be just or tyrannical.

The Philosopher—
The Hawk and the Sparrows

At times one can see a flock of sparrows tormenting a hawk. Even though they are small and weak, sparrows in a group can drive a hawk away.

The sparrows fear the hawk. He is powerful, and heavy, and his majesty is revealed when he rides the thermal. Just by extending his wings he ascends to heights a sparrow could never reach. Sparrows can only go as high as the beating of their little wings can take them.

Be like the hawk. Go to the heights. And when you descend, come swiftly, strike cleanly, and return to the heights.

Few things are more terrifying than a strong man who can control everything except himself. And on the contrary, few things are more admirable than a man who controls himself, even when it seems like things around him are out of control—think Socrates. If the constitution of a household reflects the constitution of its head, then for the household to be just, the head must be just too.

Tyrants try to pass themselves off as just. Sometimes the result is so absurd it would be laughable if it were not so hideous. This is why self-mastery is essential for keeping weight on; hypocrisy makes you look foolish, or worse. The moment people can take you lightly, you can be sure they will. Don't give them a reason to. Children have a way of growing up, and sons in particular will be in a position to challenge you sooner than you may realize. If you have been a tyrant, you may find out the hard way that you are also a fool.

Knowledge

Where does self-mastery begin? According to the Oracle at Delphi it begins with the dictum, *Know Thyself*. Without self-knowledge you'll never master your passions because you will never be able to separate yourself from them.

When it comes to knowledge strive to be a guru. In Sanskrit a guru is a man who is so heavy with knowledge that he can dispel shadows. That's because that's what *guru* means—*heavy*. (Two languages now; it looks like we may be onto something!)

The Delphic oracle counsels us to know ourselves first. So far, so good; but how do we go about it? Can we learn anything about ourselves from our armchairs? Yes, a good deal actually—but only if time in the armchair is broken up by time on your feet doing things. Think about it this way: you can only learn whether you're honest or not by trying to tell the truth. Likewise, you'll only know whether you are courageous or not by attempting daring-do. If you sit around doing nothing until you've learned enough about yourself to attempt something, you won't learn much and you won't get much done. Conversely, if you're just an unthinking doobie, you won't learn much either. You must do both: think and act, act and think. Then do it again.

Now, let's move on from self-knowledge: you should become a people watcher. There are things we all share in common, but there are also things that distinguish us from others. The more you master yourself, the more you may feel tempted to look down on other people. I assure you, this would be a mistake. It could ruin you. It also demonstrates that you really don't know yourself as well as you should. Self-mastery is good for you and the people around you; pride is not. Pride is actually a form of ignorance. There is no quicker way to shed moral weight than through contempt.

In order to put yourself in the shoes of people very different from yourself you'll need a good imagination. The world looks very different to a 300-pound wrestler than it does to someone in a wheelchair. But you're not just trying to imagine what it feels like to be someone else. What you really want to understand is what different sorts of people can contribute to you and to others.

The reason is that the head of a house puts people to work. You're not trying to manipulate anyone, quite the reverse—you're trying to serve people by giving them useful things to do, things that they can enjoy and take a wholesome pride in. And you're trying to build them up even as you build up your household.

Finally, there are basic skills—you really must master some. We've all seen those television commercials where a beautiful woman gets out of a car to check the engine, leaving some poor loser to watch. While we may feel some admiration for the woman (no one ever looks down on someone for knowing how to do something—at least no healthy person does) even the most politically correct person will feel some contempt for the guy in the car.

If you want to keep the weight on, don't be that guy. Now you can't do everything, but it is possible to become very good at a few useful things, and passably competent at several things. So, what should you focus on?

Use this as your divining rod: *Is this a skill that will help me acquire, and hold onto productive property?* (No, I never tire of beating that drum.)

Since I own both investment real estate and write books, the properties that I hold call for two somewhat different skill sets. When it comes to taking care of my real estate there are some things I'm good at—carpentry for instance, both rough and finish; I'm also pretty good at finish work: sheet rock, painting, and the like. I've got enough rudimentary knowledge to wire a house or plumb a bathroom. And over the years I've had more than 40 tenants and have been involved in roughly 100 real estate deals—so I'm a fair negotiator. I'm also a pretty good judge of property value. Communication is one skill that carries over from writing to real estate—so, I'm pretty good at putting my thoughts into words. And that's very important when it comes to working with tenants, subcontractors, agents (both realtors and literary agents), and lawyers. Another thing that is useful with both worlds is decisiveness. I don't know if that is a skill per se, but it is indispensible. I have had to hire people and had to fire people, I've signed hundreds of contracts, and I have evicted tenants. And many of these skills are transferable to other things besides publishing and real estate. Naturally, when it comes to any of these things in my household, I dispel the shadows—I am the guru.

The Paterfamilias—Sometimes a Heavy Must Hide His Weight

A grave man must be feared without being resented. Even the heaviest man can be overcome by the weak if they attack in sufficient numbers. Mobs are like violent weather—short-lived (thankfully), but temporarily inexorable.

The heavy is feared because of his power to harm; he is envied because the weak wish to be powerful; yet he can be loved if he knows how to hide his weight.

What to do? The best solution, if it can be managed, is for the heavy to hide himself in the interests of the weak. The heavy makes himself secure by only showing his weight in ways that help to secure their interests. And there must be an economy to such a display—enough to accomplish, but not so much as to engender resentment. In this way the interests of the heavy and those of the weak are reconciled.

Glory

Now I come to something that the cultural relativists among my readers—trusting that a few are still with me—will write off as just another coincidence. In the Bible, *glory* is heavy.

The Hebrew word for glory is *chabod*. The word actually is translated as *heavy* in certain contexts. And speaking of context, you may have run across chabod elsewhere. Put the letter "I" in front of it and you get *ichabod*, which means, *the glory has departed*. You also get the first name of the silly protagonist in Washington Irving's short story *The Legend of Sleepy Hollow*—Ichabod Crane. Which makes sense: Crane is a comic figure.

Counter-intuitively, in the Bible God's glory is evidenced by a cloud—a luminous, billowing cloud of crushing weight. (When the glory enters Solomon's temple, everyone falls to his knees.) And also in the Bible, when it comes to items used in worship, gold is often the material they're made with. That's because its heft, when combined with its luster, says: *glory*.

There isn't much purchase for this sort of thing in many churches these days. That's why so many of my colleagues try to keep things light; those Hawaiian shirts and flip-flops many of those mega-church pastors wear are intended to put people at ease—to make the minister likable. Perhaps that's one reason why so few people take them seriously.

What's this mean to you? Simple: *glory lends you weight*.

It has something to do with your reputation, but there's more to it than that. There is a purity to glory, where gravitas is essentially moral weight. When it comes to glory, justice and purity are included in the mix. And this is what makes it precious. When you see it, there is no arguing with it. In the Bible when people see the glory of the Lord they're dumbfounded. You can find evidence for the same thing outside the Bible. Here is an example from one of the most popular works of literature in the world—*The Lord of the Rings*.

If you have read Tolkien's classic, you may recall that a hobbit named Bilbo Baggins has a beautiful magic ring. During the course of the story it is revealed that the ring is evil and will, over time, corrupt anyone in possession of it. Bilbo's old friend Gandalf the wizard tries to persuade the hobbit to hand it over for his own good. As evidence that the ring already has a baleful influence on Bilbo, the hobbit accuses the wizard of trying to steal it. This leads to the following confrontation.

> "Well, if you want the ring yourself, say so!" cried Bilbo. "But you won't get it. I won't give my precious away, I tell you." His hand strayed to the hilt of his small sword.
>
> Gandalf's eyes flashed. "It will be my turn to get angry soon," he said. "If you say that again, I shall. Then you will see Gandalf the Grey uncloaked." He took a step towards the hobbit, and he seemed to grow tall and menacing; his shadow filled the little room.

> Bilbo backed away to the wall, breathing hard, his hand clutching at his pocket. They stood for a while facing one another, and the air of the room tingled. Gandalf's eyes remained bent on the hobbit. Slowly his hands relaxed, and he began to tremble.
>
> "I don't know what has come over you, Gandalf," he said. "You have never been like this before. What is it all about? It is mine, isn't it? I found it, and Gollum would have killed me, if I hadn't kept it. I'm not a thief, whatever he said."
>
> "I have never called you one," Gandalf answered. "And I am not one either. I am not trying to rob you, but to help you. I wish you would trust me, as you used." He turned away, the shadow had passed. He seemed to dwindle again to an old grey man, bent and troubled."

"Gandalf the Grey uncloaked." What a curious statement. What did he mean?

The shadow tells us—Bilbo would have seen Gandalf's glory in all its justice and purity crashing down upon him. That's the weight of glory.

Chapter Nine

Piety

Houses are practical things that meet basic needs. They are supported by things that are easy to justify, things like productive property, strong bonds between the sexes, fair-dealing—those things. Add to this the strong likelihood that the institutions that have replaced them in our time will let us down in the near future and it may seem like there is no need for a higher justification for bringing back the functional household.

But that is not the case. Human beings tend to look for the easy way out. And building a house is not easy. Add to this the fact that households often fail to live up to the ideals I describe in this book and it appears that we will need something more to keep us on task.

For a household to keep at it, its members must believe that their sacrifices fit into a larger structure of meaning. Helping them see that larger framework is what household piety is for.

If that seems odd to you it may be because you have come to think of piety—if you think about it at all—as a private matter, something deeply personal and inward. And it is, and always has been; but the difference between our time and earlier times is people once saw a connection between the inner self and the outer world. Today we try to keep those things separate.

Many of our ancestors believed that a person's inner world ought to reflect the outer world. The impious person was out of accord with his society. Works of piety: worship, confession, good works, etc., were all designed to maintain a harmony between the inner self and the social order and even the cosmos, especially the cosmos. And households didn't just hand this over to religious institutions. A household was a religious institution.

What Happened?

It is a long and convoluted story, but something momentous happened in the late Middle Ages that changed the world, in some ways for the better, but in other ways for the worse: *consciousness and the cosmos got a divorce.*

Religion turned away from the world, and piety became, as Alfred North Whitehead put it, *what an individual does with his own solitariness.* Even for some Christians religion has become little more than *a personal relationship with Jesus.* (Often it is even framed as an antithesis: i.e., "Christianity isn't a religion, it's a relationship.") Jesus is someone to know inwardly, not through the church: with its doctrines and sacraments. The religions that thrive today smell of Gnosticism. The reason is easy to see: the physical world has been downgraded from something that proclaims the glory of God to mere stuff. It also makes it easier to live with Darwinism. Darwinism seems to confirm the gnostic conviction that the material world is either illusory or evil—something not to learn from but to conquer.

Reconnecting Meaning to Life

Since the divorce, people have had a hard time finding objective meaning. Meaning is now something that is supposed to well up from within. Instead of discovering it, we make it, or at least we think we do. Among the many problems with this is that meaning is now privatized. For a while it was thought that our minds had enough in common with other minds that shared meaning was still possible. Hardly anyone believes that anymore.

A very influential set of people think that we should focus solely on practical concerns. We shouldn't depend on a higher truth to guide us. All we should be concerned with is survival; that and making people as comfortable as possible. You could say that my panegyric to the traditional household to this point has had something of this flavor. But now I've come to a place where that won't do. We need something that can transcend our time, especially if our time gets hard.

Do We Live In a Machine?

Since the divorce we've come to think of nature as a vast machine. The fact that most people today don't see that this is merely a metaphor shows how much has been lost. Even so there is an irony to this. After all, machines are made by people to serve them and are therefore meaningful.

So here we are: meaning is believed to reside solely in the mind; but our minds exist in a meaningless machine-like universe. This isn't very tenable really; something has got to give. And it has. Consciousness is giving ground to the machine.

In the past materialists more or less left the mind alone. While they have always believed you could reduce the mind to matter, they didn't have the wherewithal to prove it. Today we have the technology to peer into the brain. Now consciousness is no longer a safe haven from materialism. The race is on to prove that the mind is nothing but the software for the hardware in our heads.

Can Machines be Pious?

Everything people make reflects what they believe in; if we believe the world is a meaningful place then we make things that reflect that. But if we think we live in something meaningless, then everything we make will reflect *that*.

The champions of the machine are winning. Meaninglessness has seeped into everything: the universities obviously, but also the arts, politics, business, and even religious institutions. Since religious institutions were established for the sole purpose of revealing the hidden meaning of reality, this is a problem. Some religions are committing suicide in slow motion. Even ostensibly conservative religions have turned inward. They have left the world for others to define. As a result it is getting harder for conservatives to find a place in the world. Things are even worse for religious liberals because they have made themselves superfluous.

> *The Philosopher—*
> *A Few Kind Words for Religion*
>
> The word *religion* comes from the Latin for *bind*. Now that sounds just terrible to the modern ear. But it all depends on what you mean. What about being bound to your family and friends?; how about being bound to God?; aren't those bonds good things? That's how people once thought about religion. In all cultures, and at all times, religion was a glue that helped to hold a society together.

Prospects for Households

Households will not last if they are merely little islands of meaning in a sea of meaninglessness.

But is the universe nothing more than a meaningless machine? Perhaps there is an older way of seeing the world that was never truly disproved but merely passed out of fashion. And there is; I've been alluding to it for pages. The universe is not a machine; it is a cosmos.

Creation Is a Temple

When some people read the creation story in Genesis they mistakenly take it to mean that human beings are the point of it all.

There are a couple of problems with doing that. For one thing, there are vast regions unfit for human habitation: the sea for example, the heavens for another. Now these regions are inhabited by creatures fit for them: fish, birds, and even more exotic things. But these places are not fit for us.

Second, we're given a glimpse of God visiting these regions. He wades in the sea; he rides upon the storm. In visions both playful and terrifying we see an outsized-world enjoyed by an even more outsized-God. And this long before the invention of the telescope. What is it all about?

Well, we've missed the obvious. We've been given a place, but it isn't the only place. There are other places for other creatures. But there is one being who can enjoy all these places, and that's God Almighty.

Throughout scripture creation is depicted as an immense house. It has a lower floor for things that we can see—everything from forests to galaxies—but it also has an upper floor for things we cannot see. (That's even true for the sky. In days gone by the wise considered the sky just the underside of the heavens.)

These two floors made up creation visible and invisible. But one is situated over the other; the invisible rules the visible. God rules from an invisible upper story. Heaven is his throne, and the earth, (where we build our houses), is his footstool. (Isaiah 66:1)

The Paterfamilias—
A Stairway to Heaven

People have built stairways to heaven since Nimrod. That's what ziggurats were and every major city in the ancient Near East had one of them.

The problem is that our ladders don't actually reach heaven. One has to be lowered down from above. That's what Jacob witnessed with his famous ladder (Genesis 28:12). He dreamed that he saw a stairway to heaven and angels going up and down it. Angels are messengers of course (that's what the name *angel* means). The implication is that they were carrying messages down from above and prayers up from below.

How Temples Work

Templesare houses for very special occupants. They are dwelling places for gods. Today that is easy to miss but it would have been impossible to miss once. When we think of temples, if we do at all, we think of them as places where people do religious things. When people are absent, no one is home. Again, that wasn't what people thought in the old days; in those days if the god wasn't home no one would have bothered to go to a temple.

Something else about temples: they are a home away from home. A temple is actually a small-scale replica of the god's true home—more virtual reality than the real thing. What a temple is supposed to do is bring you mystically into the presence of the deity. So, in a sense, you could say the god is always at home and yet never really at home at the same time.

Solomon's Temple

When it came to the way a temple should work you could say the Israelites were on the same page with their neighbors. God had his true home—one he had built for himself; but he also had a little replica in Jerusalem.

Of course Solomon's temple was different from other temples in remarkable ways. For one thing, there was no idol in it. In neighboring temples the idol was the thing that told you the god was at home; no idol, no god. Solomon's temple did come with a throne, a very peculiar one with a hopeful name—*mercy seat*. This was situated on top of a gold-plated box that contained three artifacts: a staff, a jar containing a mysterious substance called manna, and the Ten Commandments. These symbolized the foundation of God's rule: guidance, sustenance, and justice. But the main thing to note here is that this throne reflected a higher one in heaven.

In a sense Solomon's temple brought God's throne down to earth, but in another sense it brought the Israelites up to the real throne room—the one in heaven. The temple was a ladder. It connected the floors in God's house, the lower, visible floor, and the heavenly, invisible one.

Domestic Piety

I don't blame you if this detour through ancient religious practices has left you feeling a bit impatient. But we've finally arrived. Here's the point: our houses are what they are because they are in some small way tiny replicas of the cosmos itself.

A Ranch-Style Universe Makes for Ranch-Style Houses

Please indulge me as I take you on just one more short detour, this time through a ranch-style universe. As you probably know, a ranch style home only has one story. When it comes to the universe, people who don't believe in an upper-story (heaven) are left with the problem of explaining the order we see all around us. The current theory runs something like this: that order you perceive is actually an illusion. What we call order is really just a loss of momentum from the Big Bang. The bang got things going but what we live in is a phase in an entropic process that will continue into the distant future and finally end with something known as, "heat-death."

Now scientists will tell you that we still have a lot to learn about the physical universe. Consequently their models are provisional and open to revision. But even if scientists had all the facts they could not tell you how to live. That calls for something scientists can't study using their methods. Now there is nothing wrong with science and I have no argument with it. The problem isn't science, it is the notion that science can tell us everything we need to know about how we ought to live. This notion goes by the name of *scientism*.

What does scientism have to do with households? Everything, really. If scientism is our guide, then we will eventually conceive of our households on the model of a ranch-style universe and the best we'll be able to hope for in our houses is a balance of competing interests, not a purposeful order.

I believe this is the hidden reason our households are so unstable these days. Even as the buildings we inhabit get bigger, the number of people actually living in them seems to be getting fewer. We now have something that would have been considered an oxymoron in the old days, "the one-person household."

In a two-story cosmos, power is allied with authority. But in a ranch-style universe all you are left with is naked power. And in the end things fall apart, everyone is out for himself, and the head of the house (if there even is one) is more often resented than respected.

Nesting

Our households really are very small in the big scheme of things. Not only are they vanishingly tiny in comparison to the vastness of the universe, they are even dwarfed by human political and economic institutions.

But we can imaginatively situate them in one place or the other. Either we can make our nests beneath the sacred dome of God's house—one house nesting in another, or we can live our lives arbitrarily within the violent machinery of the modern world. Either one or the other will give us our pattern to follow.

Now, if you choose the former, and build according to the old pattern, you will find that your two-story affair will rise above the modern ranch-style homes that surround it. Your pattern of an ordered cosmos with an upper story will contrast strikingly with the chaos of competing interests that you see in ranch-style homes. This raises a problem, because unless you raise some walls, you will find it impossible to maintain the ordered purpose of your house.

The Philosopher—
Agonistics

Agonistics refers to a process by which order emerges through conflict. It should get you thinking of a related word—*agony*.

Order through conflict is now the creation myth of Western civilization. It is especially reflected in economic theories both on the right and on the left: on the right there is the creative destruction of the market, and on the left there is the economics of class warfare. But beneath them both it is not hard to discern Darwin and *the survival of the fittest*.

But these theories conflict with the biblical vision of a peaceable kingdom. Is it any wonder that even households are now arenas of competing interests?

Raising Walls

We can learn something about raising the walls from the walls that God raised when he made the cosmos. Again, back in Genesis, at the very beginning of the beginning, the Lord raised walls: he separated light from dark, the waters above from the waters below, and so forth. Then he named these distinct things. And through these moves a formless void was transformed into a cosmos. Then God entered his rest. And rest, by the way, is a reference to God *resting upon his throne*.

When you build your house you will need to raise some walls. This is the first thing to do in establishing an order. And the second is like unto it: you must give the things you have set apart their proper names. This goes straight back to the Garden. Adam's first job was to name the animals. But now you run into a problem. Your house includes other people—people with wills of their own. The perpetual threat of chaos then is not just from the outside; a fifth column can arise from within. This finally brings us back to the subject of this chapter.

The Craftsman—
Household Architecture

There are remarkable parallels between the way classical Roman houses and traditional Chinese houses were laid out. Both shielded their occupants from prying eyes. (The exterior walls were windowless.) And both were open to the sky. At the center of each was an atrium bringing in light and air from above; and in the middle of these miniature courtyards pools were set up to collect rainwater. These spaces were functional as well as beautiful, filled with vegetables and herbs, and in the case of the Chinese house the pool even contained fish. The rooms that surrounded the atrium in both houses tended to serve a single purpose and were strongly differentiated. Members knew their places, and rooms tended to reflect the relative status of their occupants. The entrances of these houses were designed to segregate visitors (or customers) from residents. Upon entering, a person had to pass through a series of transitional spaces, each one more private than the last.

Contrast these houses from antiquity with Phillip Johnson's *Glass House.* Johnson was an architect who spent much of his adult life building up his residence on 47 acres in New Canaan, Connecticut. As its name indicates, its exterior walls (if you can call them walls) are made of glass. And there are no interior partitions. It has what we know today as an open floor-plan.

Turns out the place was just for show. Johnson didn't actually live in it. He lived in an adjacent structure known as the *Stone House.* But the Glass House has been influential even so. Modern houses include as much glazing as can be gotten away with. And the open floor plan makes it impossible to set aside or prioritize space.

Pietas

Romans believed that piety is the glue that holds things together—even the structure of the cosmos itself.

The first school of piety was the household. Roman coins sometimes depicted a grown child carrying his elderly father on his back (a reference to Virgil's *Aeneid*, which tied Rome's origins to ancient Troy). The father once carried the child; now the child carries the father. Although piety looks back, paradoxically it also looks forward. The coins show the son carrying his father into the future. He cares for him for a time, but his burden is set down at the father's death. He then takes up another, the obligation to honor his father's memory and to extend his line. In Roman houses a bust of the founding father, sometimes his death mask, was kept above the hearth, just as a reminder.

But piety didn't stop there. It moved in other directions: further back to ancestors, outward to civil authorities—and even to the natural world—but especially upward to heavenly things. Household piety included all that, but it began with honoring parents.

Household Piety in Three Difficult and Counter-Cultural Steps

We have finally arrived at a to-do list. Generally I'm not a big believer in these. The problem with to-do-lists is they usually fail to reveal the assumptions that they're based on. Piety, as it was understood in classical times, is so counter-cultural today I had to spend pages getting to this point, otherwise you might have rejected all I am about to recommend without understanding the reasons for the recommendations.

> *The Craftsman—The Wise Man Built His House Upon a Rock*
>
> Jesus ended the *Sermon on the Mount* with a little story about two house builders (Matthew 7:24–27). The first builder (revealingly called *The Fool*) builds his house on sand. The second, called *The Wise Man*, builds his house on rock. Then there is a storm. The first house falls flat but the second stands firm. Then Jesus made an application—if you follow my teaching you will be the second sort of man.
>
> There is a reality that we must conform to it if we have any hope that our efforts will have lasting results. The wise man knows what is solid and what is not. He knows the difference between truths and falsehoods, realities and illusions. He builds on rock, not on sand.

First, Set Yourself Apart.

Returning to the two-story cosmos theme—you must build a second-story to your house and then you must enter the second story and live there. It is from this location that you will govern your house. Before I go any further let's get something straight: you don't do this because you're especially intelligent, or talented, or better than other people. You do it because it is your role. The role isn't significant because you are—you are significant because your role is.

As with real estate, it comes down to location. No one else can stand in your place. In order to honor the past, or what is above, people in your house will need to pass through you to do so. It is simply a matter of where you are in relationship to these things. You come between.

You ought to detect something old and even heraldic here. You play a symbolic, even quasi-sacramental role in the hierarchy of the cosmos. You are the priest of your house.

You are the first of many layers. The role you play in conveying the meaning of life to those beneath you is inestimable. Even social science—at least in one respect—supports the wisdom of this. Believe it or not, studies demonstrate that fathers have a greater influence on the formation of our beliefs than mothers. And this is true for girls as well as boys. This means you cannot delegate the task of inculcating household piety to your wife—not because she lacks intelligence or desire—but because in the very act of delegating it you communicate something to your children. You say that piety is not important enough for a father to deal with directly.

Second, Honor Others

The Ten Commandments locate the honor due to parents just below the worship we owe to God and just above the regard we owe our neighbors. Parents are like middlemen then, mediating honor to the world above the house, and to the world beyond it.

This is why you shouldn't be shy about expecting the honor due to you—not because it serves as a kind of ego-trip, but because it is through you that the members of your household will learn to honor God and neighbor. But here's the trick—indirection is key. Often it is the first to demand respect that's last to get it. The following practices may help you to secure honor, but through a backdoor.

You may be like me, a child abandoned by his parents. If that is the case, you can think of yourself as the beginning of a new line—like Abraham. When the Lord identifies himself in the Bible he begins with Abraham, not with Abraham's father. Omissions can say a lot. Abraham made for a fresh start; you can be a fresh start too. But this leaves you at a disadvantage. To whom do you give honor?

Honor your failed parents if you can; honor someone else's parents if you cannot. Certainly you can honor your wife's parents if they qualify. That's what I try to do.

I'm not saying that honorable parents must be moral exemplars in every respect. If we limited honor in that way we'd hardly have anyone left to honor. But honorable parents have done their duty: protected, fed, and educated their dependents, labored honestly and obeyed the laws.

Next, you should honor your wife. Keep in mind that since she is your body, her honor reflects well on you. (The same is true for her, when she honors you as her head, it reflects well upon her.) Naturally, it is easier to honor your wife if she honors you. But if you do not have such a wife, honor her anyway.

Naturally, you should honor all those in authority—even when you disagree with them. It may be especially important to do so when you don't. Don't take it for granted that the members of your house will always agree with you! And finally, honor the Lord your God—in his house as well as yours. Ultimately your authority comes from him; fail to honor him and you may find that the members of your house will fail to honor you.

Third, Institute and Guard Symbols of Authority

You must insist on titles, especially for people other than yourself. And when it comes to you, feign hearing loss when unused. In our slovenly day, *Dad* is acceptable. If the world manages to get on its feet again, we may see a revival of *Father*. All other adults should be *ma'am* and *sir*. Should it happen that some adult eschews such respect and says to your child something like, "Mr. Johnson is my father—call me Bob!" you ought to take him aside and let him know the ground rules with your children. If Bob can't handle adulthood, don't let your children spend time with him. Your children graduate to first names with grownups when they can vote, drive, and serve in the army.

Speech is only half the game; the other half is setting aside times and places. You really must set aside some space in the house for yourself. Make it prominent and central. If it comes with a door, great—use it. When I bought the house we currently live in, it had nothing like this. It had one of those casual, open floor plans, without spaces set apart, all things being equal and accessible. The wife and kids liked the house and it is in a good location, so I bought it. Anyway, since I'm a builder I knew I could add what it needed, and that's just what I did.

I put in an office. I gave it a vaulted ceiling (the only one in the house), a built-in desk with storage, and windows all around to take in the property. Then I crowned it by putting in a large leather chair. Everyone knows this is my office and that this is my chair. I have other chairs in the house: the one at the head of the table for example, and another leather chair by the hearth. Here's something that just occurred to me as I am writing this—I have never walked in on one of my children, or even my wife, sitting in one of my chairs. And I don't recall ever telling them they shouldn't. They just don't.

Finally, you must become inaccessible on a regular basis. People and things that are too accessible are taken for granted. I learned this lesson years ago at an auto show. All the new models were on display, including those of the luxury brands. Not having much experience with high-end automobiles I went from make to make, opening them and taking a seat. And as I did, their mystique wore away; that is, until I came to one make which I'm sure you'd recognize by name. Its doors were locked. To get into one of them, you had to ask permission. They knew how to set themselves apart.

To inspire awe you must do the same thing. Now, what you do during these private times is not as important to those on the outside as the fact that they are on the outside. Even your wife should ask permission to enter. I recommend using the time for scripture, or great books, or even planning the day.

The Light From the End of the World—the Last Homely House

I could close the subject here if it were not for a door that someone has left open at the end of the world. There is light shining back to us from that direction. By that light we can see that there is more to our lives than our households can contain.

We will outlive our houses; why, we will even outlive the cosmos. Scripture promises that we will be raised and given new bodies to inhabit as well as a new world to live in.

There will be a new household too. Some of the rules that apply now won't apply to it. The Lord told us so. For one thing, he informed his disciples that there will be no marriage in the Kingdom of Heaven, that our wives will be more like sisters. And there will be only one house, with one head—and it won't be you or me.

This means we live in temporary accommodations. Our world is more like a trailer park than a real neighborhood. If you've ever been inside a trailer you know nothing in it is built to last. A trailer is a home away from home and it is designed to make you comfortable for a time.

The fact that there is an open door at the end of the world means that our households must be open ended too. We cannot define anyone exhaustively—there is something more to say, but it is not for us to say. Religions that imagine an afterlife for our households are in for a big surprise. A husband is never simply a husband; a wife is never merely a wife. Our children do not belong to us. Everyone has a future that extends beyond the doorway at the end of the world. Nevertheless, the roles we play here, even though they are temporary, are real because they reflect in a real way what we will know in the light of that eternal day when the kingdom finally comes.

Now, the bridge that connects the houses we live in today, and the one we will dwell in someday, is the Church. It is the witness to and even an inchoate embodiment of that eschatological household. It has one foot in this world, and the other in the world to come. It teaches us the meaning of this world (promoting gratitude for it and showing us how to glorify God here) but all the while it reminds us that this is not our final resting place. It shows how the very institutions that make life livable here actually serve as signs, pointing to the world to come.

Part IV

Outside the House

Chapter Ten

The Principalities

In the musical, *Fiddler on the Roof*, an earnest student asks, "Rabbi, is there a proper blessing for the Czar?" The rabbi answers, "A proper blessing for the Czar? Of course. May God bless and keep the Czar—far away from us."

When is comes to government the adage: *Can't live with it, can't live without it* seems apropos. People in the past were clear-eyed about this. Minorities, like those Russian Jews celebrated in *Fiddler on the Roof*, never felt a temptation to trust the government too completely. Governments are Janus-faced things, looking after your interests with one face, while pursuing their own with the other.

In most of the world, what people expect of their governments is corruption. In the United States we still live in the afterglow of the town meeting, where free and responsible citizens deliberated for the common good. But the glow is fading.

As I pointed out earlier, states depend upon households for a healthy social order, yet they compete with households for the devotion of their citizens. Governments find it easier dealing with unencumbered individuals than with well-structured households. Yet we still have laws that presume a household-centered way of life. But many of those laws have been written off as retrograde, or they're ignored. As a result, any man attempting to build a house on the model I have been describing may feel that the world is against him.

Give Honor to Whom Honor is Due

When law and liberty are on good terms with each other you have something called *ordered liberty*. One alternative to this is anarchy. (The other alternative is tyranny.) Now anarchy is not your friend—it's a remorseless whirlwind that will tear your house apart. For ordered liberty we need good government, and that means that just civil authority is a good thing.

What Are Governments For?

Small communities often get by on trust and custom, but once a community grows beyond a certain point someone must be apointed to adjudicate disagreements. And disagreements always arise—usually about who has a right to what. At the bottom then, governments secure more than public order; they secure private interests. And since productive property is especially of interest to households, it really is in your best interest to support the institutions of civil order.

Police work is the first thing to come to mind here, but the state helps you secure ownership in other ways too. Civil courts help enforce private contracts, and in the case of real estate, municipalities maintain a public record of ownership and transfer. States also oversee the transfer of wealth from one generation to another. (If you have ever been privy to family discord at the reading of a will you should be able to see how the state can be a friend and ally to household order.)

John Locke famously said that states should secure, "life, liberty, and property." Thomas Jefferson for some reason decided to substitute, "the pursuit of happiness" for property. This may be one of the reasons why we have lost sight of just how important productive property is for both life and liberty. Under Communist regimes the state simply confiscates productive property, ostensibly making it common property. In practice though, everyone's property becomes no one's property. Or more cynically, it is de facto the property of

> *The Paterfamilias: Sojourning*
>
> Even the best-built house is merely a temporary structure. It is good to remember that Abraham, the greatest house builder of them all, lived in a tent.
>
> Why should we remember that? Because we may find ourselves dispossessed.
>
> Sometimes the governing authorities will look upon you favorably, at other times, not so favorably. Remember Abraham's great-grandson Joseph? Egypt's Pharaoh gave his family the land of Goshen, but another Pharaoh took it away. Pharaohs are like that. Every house is a tent, and every householder is a sojourner and a pilgrim in this world.

bureaucrats and the politically connected. But even in a democracy property can be confiscated by degrees over time.

Blest Be the Ties that Bind

We really are feeble, dependent creatures who rely upon each other for everything we need. We are cast into the world by the hand of God but we are received into it by other hands. We have no choice in the matter when it comes to these people. But fair is fair; these people don't get to choose us either. They're bound to care for us, hopefully by cords of affection—and in a healthy political order, also by law and social custom. I hope you see what I'm driving at—our houses are bound together by these cords. States should encourage us to honor them—especially the un-chosen ones.

Unfortunately modern welfare states tend to do just the opposite: they weaken household bonds. (I'm not saying this is the intent, but it is the effect.) When someone becomes burdensome, often there is a government agency ready to relieve us. Now there are even laws that permit us to server bonds at the beginning of life and at its end through abortion on demand and euthanasia. But these are only the more controversial ways that welfare states tend to weaken household bonds. Even without these laws, the overall trend is to shift the burden of responsibility away from households and onto states. Households have lost their significance, along with the loyalty of their members.

The Lines Have Fallen for Me in Pleasant Places

Years ago an Ethiopian friend (who happened to have a PhD from Harvard) shared a humorous story with me. One day his two children declared, "You can't tell us what to do, this is America!" To which he responded, "America ends and Ethiopia begins right at that door!" You need to find your own way of saying the same thing, but don't expect the state to help you.

Walls are good; you need them more than ever today. They're what make you, *you*. And they also make what's yours, *yours*. It is a bit chicken and egg. You don't raise walls because you have something to protect; you have something to protect because you already have walls. And when it comes to the state, you must let the state know where it ends and your household begins.

But there is no reason to make unnecessary enemies in the process. Here are two things you can do to win some friends.

Get Out More

Tip O'Neill used to say, "All politics is local." O'Neill was one of those old-school politicians from Boston. I'm not sure how many people would agree with him today. Local politics is often considered a stepping-stone to bigger things. Perhaps it was always that way, but my guess is the impulse is stronger today. But this may be what gives you your opportunity. Local politics is where a householder should feel most at home.

Being on good terms with your neighbors is especially a good idea when you're a bit odd. And if you take the advice contained in this book to heart, you will be odd. One way to be on good terms with your neighbors is by contributing to the common good.

In a world that changes rapidly, where people move around too much and are too slow to settle down, where anonymity is the norm and movement is mistaken for progress, communities need more sticks-in-the-mud. What noncommittal types learn too late is that genuine freedom is more a matter of agency than choice. And agency comes with staying put and getting to know people.

There are many facile substitutes for agency: signing a petition, putting a bumper sticker on your car, even joining a protest. These things are not democracy in action; they often smack of mobocracy. Mobs are carried along by social-currents—by fads and groupthink. People don't rush into the streets because they know something important; they rush into the streets because they *don't know* someone important. When you know someone important, you don't stage a protest—you schedule an appointment.

As usual, it is the road less traveled that gets you where you really want to be. The reason you never hear about it is no one can figure out a way to make money from telling you about it. Here's a tip, stay put and contribute to the common good. If you do that, you may actually become the person that others come to when something needs doing. In the old days it was called, being a pillar of the community.

Property and Staying Put

It is because pillars don't move around that people depend upon them. Productive property can help you stay put. As I said before, usually it is cumbersome: real estate, a small business—those things aren't portable.

When you acquire productive property, your welfare gets bound up with the welfare of the community where it is located. This is why stable and vibrant communities are often made up of many small property-owners. When a town is dominated by a few large businesses, it may appear to be the picture of health in the good times, but beneath the surface you have unhealthy dependency. These communities very often rely upon economic forces beyond their control. When those forces shift, and businesses move away, these communities get reduced to poverty.

The Curmudgeon: Crony Capitalism

Ever hear the saying: *What's good for General Motors is good for America?* Most politicians agree with it. Big government loves big business, and vice versa. Don't be fooled by superficial acrimony: the functionaries of each go to the same dinner-parties.

A nation of smallholders is a land of modest ambitions. This is why big government loves big business: it funds its ambitions. And in return, big business gets favorable treatment. So who suffers? The little guy does. When the big boys are in cahoots they have a way of cutting off light and air from the rest of us through regulation. Contrary to the received wisdom, regulations are good for big business because they raise the price of entry for new competitors. Big business can usually afford compliance. Backing regulations on your own industry can help to increase market share as other smaller and weaker businesses are priced out of business. Regulations work great for big government too because they are ostensibly in the public interest (and sometimes they are), but they also increase the size and power of government because someone has to enforce the rules. And what bureaucrat doesn't want to be more powerful?

Contribute to the Common Good

When you have an interest in a community you share a good in common with other people. So how do you promote that good? Here's a suggestion, begin by looking for places where your interests overlap with those of others. And don't wait for a controversy before you begin. Most people don't consider holding a sign at election time a real contribution. Depending on the sign, some people may even consider it divisive. Now, you may need to take a stand at some point on some controversy, and doing so may cost you friends—but don't lose them before you even make them. And who is more likely to listen to you when a divisive issue comes up for debate, the people who know you and (hopefully) respect you, or the people who don't?

So begin with dull-normal things—like a library fundraising drive, or a main street beautification project. Take a job no one wants and everyone knows needs done. If you do that, people learn your name. And if you're reliable, people will come to depend upon you. And once that happens you'll have agency.

Mind Your Own Business

Although you should contribute to your community, don't overdo it. The interests of your household and the interests of your community do not always converge. And when some fit of madness sweeps through the community (as inevitably happens) you may even feel the need to get out of Dodge.

In our increasingly interconnected world local economies are subject to powerful forces that they cannot control. A big retail store moves to town and the already weakened Main Street finally gives up the ghost. (I've seen it.) The local high school institutes the latest fad in education, not because parents, or even local teachers, want to but because bureaucrats in Washington, D. C. mandate it. Small towns and traditional working-class urban neighborhoods have a hard time resisting these forces—and even when they try, the apologists for the powerful label them benighted or worse. Local communities can help households, but don't expect them to save you. There may come a time when your household will need to look after itself.

Now let's look at some tactics for doing just that. Each of them is intended to help you retain as much control of your interests as possible.

Convert Earned Income into Passive Income

Taxation isn't a necessary evil; it's just necessary. Taxes help to secure your interests by underwriting the public record, the civil and criminal courts, and law enforcement. But we have to keep an eye on the people who are looking out for us because government bureaucracy tends to grow to the limit it is allowed to grow. Every bureaucrat wants a bigger budget, more staff, and more power to look after you.

For this reason (among others) householders should favor limited government. We ought to treat governments like bonsai trees—daily pruning making beautiful. But, how can householders do that?

First, you should keep your money out of the taxman's hands in the first place. There are legitimate ways to do that.

If I were to offer you $1,000 to read a book on the tax code, you'd probably do it gladly, but if I promised you that you could cut your tax bill by $1,000 by reading the same book, you probably wouldn't do it. Here's what you would learn if you read the book: the amount of income you receive and the amount of tax you owe are not directly related. Tax is determined by *the ways* your income is received, *not by how much* you receive.

Here's an example of what I'm talking about: whenever money changes hands, the taxman sticks his hand out. So, whenever you realize the value of an asset (when you cash it in) there's the taxman. Let's say you own stock in a public company that has shot up in value—the moment you realize the gain by selling it you have created, as the taxman says, a *taxable event*. Now if you had simply held on to it, no tax would be due.

But what good is an asset to you if you can't derive income from it? Who said you can't? There are ways to make these things work. Allow me to welcome you to the promised land of *passive income*.

The term *passive income* is a little misleading. Passive income takes plenty of work to realize. What makes it passive is the fact that it cannot be classified as *earned income*. Confused? Don't be; the principle is actually pretty easy to understand. Rent from an apartment building is a good example of how this works. You own the building; it requires time, thought, and even physical labor to maintain; nevertheless it produces passive income. Why then is it called passive income? Because you can hire people to do the work and any profit above and beyond expenses is yours to keep. Investment real estate is only one form of passive income, a business is another. Passive income can be derived from other things: intellectual property, dividend-generating stock, interest income on loans made, derivatives. It is just a matter of making your assets work for you.

Prepared for another dose of reality? Here it is—people either *own assets* that generate passive income for them, or they *work for* the people who do. It really is that simple. Both receive income, but people who receive passive income are taxed at a lower rate than people who receive earned income.

If that doesn't seem fair that is probably because you don't understand why earned income *must* be taxed at a higher rate. Think about it this way: what happens to an employee when he gets sick and cannot go to work? He receives unemployment benefits, maybe even Social Security, right? Where does the government get the money for those things? Taxes. Social Security tax is just one form those taxes take. While it is true that employers help to pay both Social Security and Medicare taxes (they must match an employee's contribution) for the employer this is just another cost of doing business. It is another deduction on income. The passive income that remains after business expenses are paid are not subject to these taxes. The reason is the owner of the asset can still derive income from a property whether he can work or not. For an employee, when the work stops, so does the income.

Make Government Redundant

There is an old television commercial about the Maytag repairman. The gist of it was that the repairman had nothing to do because the washing machines he serviced were so well made they never broke down. The principle transfers well: if you want the government to become as much like the Maytag repairman as you can make it, give it as little to do as possible. And don't let it entice you with promises to relieve you of your burdens. Keep doing those things because governments are really good at hiding their costs, usually through debt. There's no free lunch—you'll always pay. But maybe the greatest cost of government services is the way that they sap your strength. In the weightlessness of outer space muscles shrink and bones atrophy from lack of use. Remember this when the government says, "Let us relieve you of that burden."

Here's a puzzler: does social decay beget government growth or does government growth beget social decay? (Probably both.) No matter where you come down on that issue though, I hope at least that you agree with me that there will eventually come a day when the government can no longer do all the things we have come to expect it to do. Get ready for that day.

Two areas where households can regain some of their strength right away are child-care and eldercare. The more we can reintegrate these back into our households the more difficult we make it for states to justify their social services in these areas.

Historically, women have shouldered the burdens for these things. Don't be fooled though, even though we now farm these things out to the state, women still do most of the work—they just don't do it from home or for people they love. And women are likely to continue doing most of this work (unless women are replaced by robots).

One of the ways our society shames women into taking these services out of the house and into the "workplace" is by equating a paycheck with real work. The implication is that work done for love is less significant than work done for money. Fortunately an increasing number of women have learned through bitter experience the meaning of wage slavery. Still, as heads of house we need to do a better job of honoring our mothers and daughters when they perform this often difficult and frustrating work. If the prosperity of our houses is of first concern, and everyone gets a fair share, then our wives and daughters will be working for themselves even as they work with us. And if building our houses fully occupies us as men, they won't feel we've left them behind.

Defend Yourself

Monopolies are always bad for you, but when it comes to coercive force, a state monopoly can kill you. This is why householders tend to support the right to bear arms. It may seem counterintuitive, but domestic tranquility is best secured through the wide distribution of coercive force—not by giving the officials in charge exclusive right to it. The police should supplement rather than replace household self-defense. And there should always be enough coercive force distributed throughout a community to hold a police force accountable. (Organizing a community for such a thing would be difficult and would only be possible if the police were guilty of horrific abuse. But horrific abuse is less likely if the police know they are not the only force around.)

In traditional societies, households are usually armed. Where the laws permit, you should be too. Where the laws do not permit it, you should work to change those laws. While you work for the right to defend yourself, prepare to defend yourself to the extent the law will allow. Turn your plows into swords and your pruning hooks into spears. Take martial arts courses. Do something, anything, to foster a mindset of household self-defense.

> *The Craftsman: Homeschooling*
>
> Compulsory public schooling has been the state's primary means of indoctrination for a century and a half now. Among its objectives is the undermining of household-based education.
>
> This being the case, the legal status of homeschooling (at least in the United States) is something like a miracle. Having been permitted for so long now, and with such a large number of successfully educated and productive citizens to its credit, it would be hard to outlaw it if these were the only considerations.
>
> But many people see public schooling as a means of socialization. And this is just what many homeschooling families want to prevent. By separating children from parents, and locating them in age-specific cohorts, public schoolchildren are made to overvalue the opinions of their peers and devalue the convictions of their parents.
>
> For those who find themselves in nation states that deny the right to homeschool, parents should educate their own children as antebellum America slaves did after dark. This requires a proactive approach, both to uncovering what the child is being taught and refuting curricula that undermine household solidarity. But if a household is to retain independence and self-determination, such deprogramming is absolutely essential.

Just owning a weapon is an education in itself. First of all, it reminds you that you do have a right to defend yourself. And like any other art, the martial arts require practice if competence is important to you. But most of all, going through the motions, whether at a gun range or in the gym, reminds you that there are dangers in the world and that you should be ready to confront them.

Your Real Enemies—Decadence and Demagoguery

Householders are not members of the middle class in the sense the term is used today. Generally the middle class doesn't own productive property in the modern world. What is owned are homes, usually mortgaged, a rapidly depreciating automobile (or two, or three), and perhaps a few mutual funds. That's about it.

Before the industrial revolution people had something else in mind when they spoke of the middle class. In those days the middle consisted of property owners: in the countryside, yeomen or husbandmen; and in the village, craftsmen, tradesmen, and small to midsized proprietors.

These were the people that Aristotle had in mind when he spoke of the middle class. And according to that philosopher, they are the basis of a free and stable society. Since they must care for themselves, they have every reason to be responsible and thrifty; and because they rely upon each other through trade and charity for their livelihoods, they're public-spirited and willing to contribute to the common good. When this class is strong, the virtues that attend them characterize the society at large.

Now, because they are in the middle that means there are people above them and below them. The upper class, then as now, tend to look down on them. And because the upper classes can afford a little decadence, they rub their decadence in the faces of the people in the middle.

Below the middle naturally there is a lower class. To the lower class the middle can either be something to aspire to join, or something to resent. In a healthy society it is the first, in a sick one, the second.

You know society has entered a decadent phase when the tastes of the upper class have supplanted the values of the middle class in the hearts of the lower class. Most of the time this occurs when the property-less contingent has swollen in size. Instead of aspiring to property ownership, these people mimic, almost comically, the decadence of those at the very top. That may be due to a loss of contact with the middle; but it probably has just as much to do with a growing dependence on government largesse. Once this phase is reached, the remnants of the true middle-class must watch out for the demagogue.

The demagogue is the man of the people—the people here being understood to be those without property. While the demagogue can rise from below, more often he is actually a member of the upper class. (Better to lead the mob than become its target.)

When the top swells with wealth, and the bottom swells with people, the end is near.

Chapter Eleven

Friendship

There was once a popular song with the line, "You and me against the world." You may feel that this book has something of that sentiment in it. I suppose that it does. But it is a matter of degree.

The household is the first institution because it binds the sexes and the generations together in a fruitful common life. At the other end of things there is the state—the largest of human institutions, binding a territory together into a single jurisdiction. But between households and states there should remain plenty of room for other institutions to exist.

Cabin Fever

You cannot find everything you need or want at home; bad things happen when you try. I'm not just thinking about the social awkwardness we see in people who don't get out enough. (Social deformation can also result from getting out too much.) What I'm thinking about here is what happens when we demand too much of the people we live with. You'll only find disappointment if you do that; the air at home will get stuffy with hurt feelings and nursed grudges. And when these things leak out, released by some small offence, they work their ways into all sorts of things. I once rented an apartment above an elderly Italian couple and their grown daughter. The girl was sickly and thin and the parents were over-cautious and controlling. The emotional atmosphere was so thick in their home that when I had to visit for some reason, I felt short of air. And I'm afraid I was an unwilling eavesdropper through the ducts to their arguments and their tears. A few years later, when I became a landlord myself, I witnessed something quite different. I bought a double-decker in an old Irish neighborhood. And tenants came with the deal. The family I inherited had lived in the smallish downstairs apartment for over 20 years and had raised three children there. Unlike the Italian landlord and family, these folks got out a lot. They were healthy, happy, and gregarious.

Welcome to yet another paradox. To be happy in our houses, we shouldn't expect too much from the people we live with. My Irish family knew each other's shortcomings and could even laugh about them—sometimes right in front of each other. They could do that because they didn't rely on each other for things they could legitimately find elsewhere. The mother belonged to a little swarm of Irish mothers that buzzed about the neighborhood, and on his way home from work each day the father dropped in at the neighborhood pub to beerily commune with friends before traipsing home. The kids were the same. They had lots of friends, and their apartment was a welcoming place, people in and out constantly. Yet, for all the traffic, there were strong bonds beneath the surface that would occasionally show through. They were loyal to each other. They knew what family is for and what friends are for, and they didn't get the two confused.

Aristotle's Three Friends

Aristotle just won't die; even after many attempts to kill him off. The reason is that he's just so exasperatingly good so much of the time. Practical too. You might even call him the first social scientist because so much of what he had to say was based on observation. His penchant for evaluating social arrangements and not merely cataloging them would probably make him *persona non grata* in social science departments today.

(By the way, social scientists are people too, with values just like the rest of us. Social scientists are often very good at disguising their moral judgments. They're so good at it that they even fool themselves.)

Friendship isn't taken very seriously today; but Aristotle took it seriously. I don't know if he made a good friend, but on the subject of friendship it is hard to find a better thinker.

He was a classifier. He gave us the basic categories we use to the present day to classify all sorts of things: genus, species, and so forth. And when it came to friendship, he identified three different types: useful friends, pleasant friends, and true friends. (I think these classifications can even apply to households—two of them anyway.) Let's look at each in turn.

Useful Friends

Useful friends are the people you form friendships with because they're useful to you. At a low level it can work like this—let's say your neighbor has a snow blower he lets you use in the wintertime and in return you let him use your brush cutter in the summer. You've got a friendship there that is useful to both of you. Now you may not have much in common with this guy—or even like him much—but according to Aristotle he's still a friend. He is a useful friend—use is the basis of the friendship; he finds you useful, and you find him the same. If you can accept this, I think you'll see that most of the people you know are useful friends. Even business dealings fit here, perhaps especially those. If someone has something I want (let's stick with snow blowers) and I have something he wants (let's say money) we can enter into a friendly exchange for mutual advantage. Our friendship may come to an end when the deal is done—or it may not—it depends on whether or not he has anything more I'd like to buy and I have any more money to spend.

This structure can even apply to institutions—it may be the only form of friendship that institutions can share. It is because households need each other that they tend to bond together to form larger communities. The first reason for doing so is pretty obvious—for a household to form in the first place, two houses need to contribute to its formation (i.e. one donating a man and the other a woman). But houses pull together for other reasons.

In Rogers and Hammerstein's musical *Oklahoma!* there is a scene in which farmers and cattlemen come together for a community dance. A song is sung entitled, *The Farmer and Cowman Should Be Friends.* But the scene ends in a fight. Farmers and Cowmen can't be friends because they want the same thing (land). They really have no use for each other; in truth, they're natural rivals. For a useful friendship to exist there must be an exchange of some kind. The land can't be shared between farmers and cattlemen—each use precludes the other. Conflict is inevitable.

This is one of the reasons that corporations can't be on truly friendly terms with households. These institutions are competing for labor and property. As corporations have come to have a near monopoly on them, households find themselves divested of the material basis of their independence. This is why most people must work for corporations and not for themselves. The result is wage slavery. Corporations and households are much like the farmers and cattlemen in *Oklahoma!* In *Oklahoma!* the fight was over land, but in our world the fight is over property and labor. Until recently it has been a rout. The corporations have been winning with ease. But that just may be changing.

Useful Friendships In the Household

The members of your household should be useful too.

For romantics this is sacrilege. They want the sweet without the bland. But a diet of nothing but sweets is cloying. Useful friendships are the bread and butter of life. This is one reason why marriages that are not useful don't last. Romantic feelings come and go. In useful marriages the parties depend on each other for the basics—the dull-normal stuff of everyday existence.

This is true when it comes to children too. Children serve no useful purpose any more. We look at a child and say, "So long as he's happy, that's all that matters"—not accounting for usefulness in our account of happiness. Perhaps this is one reason that our children disappoint us—we expect them to pursue their passions, to develop their gifts, yada, yada, yada, but we don't give them anything worth caring about. And so they shrug and they say, "Who cares?" And why should they care? And why should we be disappointed when they don't amount to anything? We preached to them the gospel of happiness, implying, without meaning to, that they have nothing worthwhile to contribute to either a household, or the world at large. So they end up worthless and miserable.

The Craftsman: Why You Should Have a Plumber Before You Need One

While it is a good thing to have a working knowledge of many things, excellence in any one thing requires time and practice. Most of the time a layman's knowledge is adequate to get by. But there are times when you need to call in an expert.

When you find a broken sewer pipe in the basement that's not a good time to go looking for a plumber. When time is of the essence, you want to know who to call and you want to feel confident that the person you call will meet the need. You also want him to know who you are, and to feel some responsibility for your welfare. Generally your crisis will likely inconvenience him. Yes, you've got sewage in the basement, but he probably has a list of other calls to make that day. Responding to you means changing his plans, maybe even rescheduling work for another customer. Now, who is he more likely to rework his day for, a stranger, or someone he knows and has worked for before?

It's wise to keep a running list of tradesmen and professionals with specialized knowledge and skills. When it comes to the skilled trades you should at least have a plumber and an electrician on the list. A general contractor or handyman is good too, maybe even an appliance repairman if you're hopeless in that department. When it comes to professionals you definitely want a doctor and a lawyer—and you maybe surprised at this one—a clergyman. File them all under the heading: *Useful Friends.*

The Paterfamilias: Hospitality

There is something known as "the hospitality industry." (It's the hotel business.) It just goes to show how far hospitality has wandered from home.

When people do bring hospitality home it means entertaining people, usually with a party. There's the host and there's the guests. We're a little closer to the original meaning of hospitality, but we're still not quite there.

If you want to see what hospitality looked like in ancient times you need to read the story of the destruction of Sodom and Gomorrah (Genesis 18–19). The episode begins with three mysterious travelers arriving at Abraham's tent. Abraham is quick to see to their needs. Later we see two of the travelers at Sodom where Lot meets them at the gate. He presses them to spend the night under his roof even though they tell him they would rather spend the night in the town square. I won't go into the lurid details here. But Lot proves to be the only righteous man in the city. As the story is told modern readers are shocked to see how far Lot is willing to go to perform his duty as a good host. But his guests relieve him of his obligation by blinding his neighbors.

This is hospitality, opening your house in order to feed and shelter people in need. It is a unilateral act of friendship that places a guest in debt to his host. There is a tacit expectation that should the guest ever find himself in a position to offer the same in return he will. Hospitality is an offer of useful friendship in which self-interest is an after thought.

When I spoke of gravitas I discouraged you from thinking of your children as friends. I'm not taking that back; what I was getting at back there is our tendency to treat them as equals. So long as they dwell in your house, and to a lesser extent, so long as you're alive, your children cannot be your equals. But they can be your friends in the very restricted sense I'm talking about here. And they should be increasingly so with time. As you age, they should care for you and make a practical return for the years of care you gave to them.

Pleasant Friends

Perhaps a reason we don't think of our communities as leagues of useful friends is because we have boiled friendship down to pleasure. We think friends are those people we enjoy being around. Their primary use is for a good time. This isn't entirely misguided.

Even here Aristotle is a helpful guide. He can show us how to derive more pleasure from our friends than we might otherwise enjoy. He tells us that friendships of this sort are formed around some pleasurable pursuit. He notes that those who enjoy music have musical friends; those who enjoy beer have beer-drinking friends; those who enjoy mountain climbing—you get it—they've got mountain climbing friends. A pleasant friendship can even find its source in something difficult to distinguish from the friend himself, like a sense of humor. If you find a friend witty, your friendship is based on a common sense of humor.

Now here's a distinction that should be made; being a pleasant person doesn't make you a friend of this type. Sure, keeping things light, being agreeable, even polite, is a good thing. Pleasantries grease the gears of social machinery. But being pleasant is not what makes someone a pleasant friend. A pleasant friend is someone you enjoy being with. And if you enjoy curmudgeonry, you want a little sourness in your friends.

It could be said that this kind of friend is the most disposable of friends. And this may be one of the reasons why modern households are so unstable. Pleasure has been made the very basis of family life. But households with staying power endure even when their members don't like each other all that much. Tastes are fickle, but basic needs are not.

Since pleasant friends come and go a household should be semi-permeable, to let them in and out. Sometimes you just need to keep certain people out. If Junior enjoys some illicit pursuit, then the friends he enjoys it with really must go away and not come back. In that case, it is essential to household health to keep Junior from forming harmful friendships in the first place.

And now for a caveat on the pleasures of pleasant friends; returning to that little Italian family I rented from so long ago, it seems to me that what they lacked were friends of this sort. I think one reason that C. S. Lewis was so gregarious was that he needed to get out. He cared for a demanding and ungrateful woman (because of a war-time promise made in a trench) and his brother (who lived with them)

The Curmudgeon: Why Your Wife Shouldn't Be Your Best Friend

When households stopped making things, the husband went from being *Producer-in-Chief* to a *breadwinner* who mysteriously disappeared for eight to ten hours a day (if not more). His wife went from being his partner in making things to *Consumer-in-Chief*. At first, cultural momentum kept childrearing at home, but we're past that now. With corporate employers and the popular media luring women into corporate work force, households are increasingly childless.

With so much of the economy now outside the home, and kids serving no real purpose besides personal gratification—what is marriage for?

In the first half of the twentieth century, when these things were still in bud, psychologists and sociologists predicted the harvest to come. Even through the haze of World War II, they could see our current world in the distance. But because marriage was still considered indispensible for a stable society, they worked to repurpose the institution and make it fit for our world. What they came up with is "Companionate Marriage." Today it is more or less what people think of when they think of marriage. Anything else seems almost unimaginable.

Companionate marriage is a recreational relationship, something for after hours, when you're off work. Instead of usefulness, emotional gratification is its foundation.

appears to have had a drinking problem. When Lewis finally did find love, he had something of the look of a drowning man. So, in a sense, enjoyed in the right way, pleasant friends may actually be indispensible.

True Friends

Now the highest form friendship can take is true friendship. This is a rare bird. It has always been hard to find, but today it may be so rare so as to qualify as an endangered species.

Hopefully it is clear by now that whenever you find two friends you actually have three things: the two people and whatever it is that binds them together. In friendship's lowest form that thing is usefulness. When that thing is pleasure, the friendship can have a short shelf life. But when that thing is goodness itself, the friendship can last in good times and bad. Devotion of this kind may even cause a person to lay down his life.

Perhaps this is the only form friendship actually takes and the other forms are just watered-down versions of the real thing. But since it can require so much from you, you just couldn't muster the energy required to maintain more than a few friendships of this type.

Now for a Little Plato

Goodness is Real

The image Plato used to convey the idea that goodness is a real thing is the sun. It's an apt image for a couple of reasons. First, the sun is impossible to look at directly. (Did anyone truly see it before the invention of filtered lenses?) Nevertheless, no one has ever doubted the existence of the sun for the simple reason that without it we couldn't see anything else. The second reason why it is a helpful image is that life itself would be impossible without it. Take away the sun and the rest of us would go with it. The sun is so real you could say it is the realest thing of all; it is necessarily real—it makes everything else possible.

Goodness is hard to separate from the things it attaches itself to. But you can do it if you think about it in the right way. Try by starting with a few undeniably good things: a good orange, a good day, a good friend. Now hold these things up before your mind's eye and pull back a little. If you do this in just the right way you'll see that you're actually looking at those things—the orange, the day, the friend—through the *concept* of good. Now that concept had to come from somewhere. Admittedly thinking like this isn't easy; the concept of good tends to be a little shy—hiding in things, lending itself to them. But a problem comes about when we fail to separate goodness from the things it inhabits. When we don't we end up over-valuing things. This is where idolatry comes from.

Goodness Can Be Measured

The goodness of a ripe tomato is different from the goodness of a child. We can say that they're both good, but not to the same degree. Some things are certainly better than the others. Follow this logic and before you know it you arrive at the conclusion that moral goodness is a very high form of goodness. And when we love the goodness of a virtuous person we can make that the basis for the best form of friendship—true friendship. Of course this assumes that a morally good person wants to be your friend, and for that to happen he must see moral goodness in you.

Getting back to Aristotle, when two morally good people form a friendship, you have the potential for a true friendship. Usefulness and pleasure usually get thrown in with this sort of friendship, but a true friendship can last even without them. True friends may enjoy skiing with each other, but if one of them can no longer ski, the friendship will survive. True friends are willing to make sacrifices for each other, to be inconvenienced, even endure hardship for each other, not because something is in it for them—they do it *for goodness sake.*

When you're talking about friendship of this sort, your wife really can be a true friend. Hopefully your children will be true friends too, along with everyone else in your household. If you are all friends of goodness, you'll be true friends in good times and bad.

Mediating Institutions

There is a way to structure friendships, even pleasant ones, so as to have them include more people than any one person can know. The way to do that is by institutionalizing the friendship. If we think about it in the right way, a private golf course can be seen as a league of friends who take pleasure in golf. In political philosophy, institutions of this kind are known as *mediating institutions*. They come between people in order to bring them together.

The term can be used in a different way. It can be used for institutions that come between individual people and the political states they reside in. Because they're in the middle they can act as a sort of buffer, keeping states from absorbing individuals, while helping individuals enjoy the benefits of life in a well-ordered state. Totalitarian states are notably lacking in these—which is why we call them *totalitarian states*—these states do everything, or at least attempt to.

Healthy societies make room for disagreement and even conflict. This is why healthy societies can be a little chaotic. When things are too coordinated there is no space for individual people to go their own ways. Mediating institutions that can resist the state make space for freedom. (Dissident political parties and non-established religions are two good examples.) You could say that in this sense a household is a mediating institution. It can shelter you from the state (among other things).

But don't forget the point I started with. People don't join mediating institutions so that they can find shelter from the state. They join them because they want to connect with other people to promote something good. Consider: art museums exist to preserve the best in the visual arts, but they also make room for art that doesn't serve the state. The same is true for everything from *The International Brotherhood of Electrical Workers* to *Little League Baseball*. The IBEW is a brotherhood of useful friends, and Little League is a league of friends committed to the pleasures of baseball.

But what about true friendship, is there a mediating institution dedicated to promoting goodness itself?

Yes, that institution is the Church. This may rub you the wrong way; you may wish to enlarge the tent to include humanitarian institutions that do things like feed the hungry or respond to natural disasters. While I am all for those things, they're one step away from what I'm getting at. Those are for good works, but they are not goodness itself. Jesus told us that goodness is only found in God. Here's why: when our minds cut themselves off from a conscious dependence upon God, goodness seems to lose its connection to anything outside the human mind. When that happens goodness is reduced to an adjective. It becomes a word we use to describe our experience of things. But if our idea of goodness has its origin in God then goodness is truly real.

The Church, Friendship, and Freedom

Households can't stand alone. And unless you live in the wilderness, you may eventually feel the full weight of the world bearing down upon you; even the best-built house will collapse under that kind of pressure. Your house needs to be reinforced by other houses. But in order for that to happen you'll need a common good—something that binds you together. And this is one place where the church comes in.

The relationship between the church and the state has always been awkward, even in the days when the church was ostensibly established. This is because the position of the church is paradoxical; it is subject to the laws of the state—just like any other entity, yet it encourages people to look over the state's head to a higher authority. And when it is believed that the state and God are at odds, the church reserves the right to disobey the state. So most of the time the church supports the state, strengthening its bonds, but at other times it is like a solvent, diluting its authority.

States like to narrow the distance between religion and civil authorities, either by compromising the authority of religion, or by making religion an organ of the state. But Christianity shouldn't cozy up to either proposition. The reason is implicit in Jesus's words, " . . . render to Caesar the things that are Caesar's, and to God the things that are God's."

The Curmudgeon: When the House of God is Hurting Your Household

It is a shame, but in many cases, the very institution that should be the biggest supporter of the household has turned against it. Churches can go bad in this regard in at least two ways.

One way is to actually undermine the symbols derived from household life that the scriptures use to understand salvation. Especially be on your guard when gender-egalitarians run the show. Certain passages from the Bible are never read, God as Father is downplayed, even the Son of God is no longer called son or even God. And submission and obedience are not merely neglected, they are attacked. New life in Christ is no longer the point; the very gospel is lost as these false shepherds affirm everything but the truth, and every lifestyle but a holy one.

Some churches do the same kind of damage by replacing household functions with church programs. A daycare center sounds like a great idea, but what is actually creating the need for the service in the first place? Sunday schools and youth groups have their places, but they can go too far, replacing rather than supplementing what should be taught at home. Churches like these may look alive, and they may even retain traditional theological language, but they may actually be draining the very life out of the households that feed them.

Chapter Twelve

Legacy

Begin with the end in mind: it's good advice. If you don't, you may find yourself following the herd to slaughter.

Keeping the end in mind should also remind you that in the end you will die. Socrates said that philosophy can be summed up as nothing but preparing for death. Someday you will be gone, and if the only person you care about is yourself, then everything you care about will die with you. I suppose that could be some solace since you would leave nothing behind that you cared about anyway. Or you could take it as a rebuke, that you really ought to strive for more, that you should leave something you care about behind. This brings me back to the beginning with the end in mind. What is it that you intend to leave behind?

There are different ways to evaluate the things we make, but one of the most important is: *How well will it hold up over time?* Most people, if they give any thought to it at all, really don't expect their households to outlive them. They think of them more as tents. But the best-built households last for generations—sometimes for hundreds of years, one for much longer.

Father Abraham Built a House

This is what the biblical patriarch Abraham managed to do. He was so successful it is sometimes a matter of violent debate determining just who his heirs are. Is it the Jews? Are Christians included? How about Muslims? They all call him father.

You could say that he got off to a slow start. He only had two sons. In a sense he lost the first, and then he nearly lost the second. On top of that he really did live in a tent and he was always on the move. And yet he founded a great house, the greatest that has ever been raised.

It should be obvious that you can't match him, and you shouldn't try. He had a lot more going for him than a book of advice, or even having the end in mind. But you can draw inspiration from his story and you can even try to live up to his example.

The Wrong Way to Rule From the Grave

Often, when people don't trust their own children, they put limits on what their heirs can do with an inheritance. One legal instrument for this goes by the counterintuitive name of, *Trust*. Some uses can be prohibited (trips to Vegas, for instance), while others are encouraged, (a college degree, for example). The problem with trusts is you treat your children like they're children. If they really are too young to handle the money when you leave this world, no problem. But if we're talking about adults, they should be free to fail. People who aren't free to fail never truly grow up.

In part the problem is a lack of wealth, not its abundance. The true wealth of a healthy household is the productive capacity of its members. If the members of your household are virtuous, then even if they lose everything, they stand a good chance of recovering their fortunes, given time.

If people lack virtue though, restrictions won't keep them in line.

A Promise

The reason that Abraham's household has endured as long as it has is because it was founded on a promise (Genesis 12:1–3). Here it is:

> "Now the Lord said to Abram, 'Go from your country and your kindred and your father's house to the land I will show you. And I will make of you a great nation, and I will bless you and make your name great, so that you will be a blessing. I will bless those who bless you, and him who dishonors you I will curse, and in you all the families of the earth will be blessed."

This is a large and wonderful promise. But the reason that it made Abraham the founder of a great house is that this is a heritable promise.

When Abraham died he left two sons but only one heir—the child born to him in his old age. He was such a delight to his parents he was named, *laughter*. (Isaac means laughter.) Certainly Abraham left the child a small fortune. But it was not as precious as God's blessing. And Isaac inherited that as well.

There is a profound lesson in this. If we want our houses to last, they will need something like Abraham's promise; something that will keep them going in good times and bad, long after we are gone.

Abraham Today

Here's a little thought experiment for you. It's pretty general, but let's give it a go anyway.

Let's say you've managed to become financially independent. You're sixty years old, you've been married to the same woman your entire adult life, and you have three grown children. You own a small business with a few employees—let's say ten—and one of them happens to be one of your sons. Your wife also works in the business as the office manager. You have a little income producing real estate on the side. One of those is the small commercial property that houses your business along with some surplus space that you lease out to a couple of other small businesses. Along with these things you own your house free and clear and you have a couple of hundred grand tied up in mutual funds. On the debt side, you've got a couple of small mortgages. Your net worth is somewhere around three million dollars. Not too shabby.

The scenario I've just outlined is pretty much within the reach of many young men in the Western world. You'd have to put your mind to it though. It would mean managing your affairs well, staying put, starting a business of some kind fairly early, taking calculated risks, and above all, having a thrifty and supportive wife. Remove any of those things and the chance of getting to this point gets less likely.

You'd also need persistence, a little frugality, some courage, and lots of common sense. What you can't give yourself is health, or a relatively stable and growing economy. But let's assume you've been healthy and that times have been pretty good.

You could take it easy at this point, cash in a few things, live comfortably, travel a bit, then leave the leftovers to your kids when you die. Your kids would then probably take the physical assets and sell them off. Then they might go on spending sprees. If they're a little better than most, they might even put some money in the bank and set up college funds for your grandkids.

But if you've truly done your job as the head of the house, you should have gotten a point across by the time your kids are grown: *productive property is precious*. It should be held on to, and added to if possible. Once liquidated, it runs off like all liquids do. If your children have seen you in action, and have gotten the message, they should be open to holding onto the assets and developing a plan that would help them do that.

So, what's the plan?

> *The Curmudgeon:*
> *The Problem of Too Much Money*
>
> Everyone has a money problem. Some people never have enough, but other people have too much.
>
> When the average person is informed that too much money can be a curse, he responds like Tevye in *Fiddler on the Roof*, "May God smite me with it! And may I never recover!" But real problems come with too much of a good thing. First, there is the problem of security; then there is the problem of where to invest it; and perhaps worse of all, there is the problem of false security that it can engender. It's cliché to say: *The first generation makes the money, the second tries to keep the money, and the third squanders the money.* Here's another: *Shirtsleeves to shirtsleeves in three generations.* The reason they're clichés is that these things are often true.

Primogeniture

If you want the work of a lifetime to last for generations you shouldn't expect probate to help with that. A will is some help, but not much. Wills are often predicated on the same assumption that guides probate judges—that assets should be liquidated to ensure a fair and even distribution capital. But if your goal is to leave a structure behind that can shelter your great grandchildren some day, you will need to pass on assets whole if you can.

Returns usually improve with scale. When we liquidate assets, we not only create a taxable event, we also winnow away our returns. Here is an example of what I mean: let's say one of your investment properties is an apartment building with twelve rental units. For simplicity's sake let's say you own the building free and clear and it generates $100,000 annually for you after taxes, insurance, and upkeep. (Not a stretch if the units rent at $1,000 each a month.) If your three heirs can leave it alone, it will generate approximately $33,300 plus in income annually for each of them. Not bad, eh? Well, let's say they can't abide the thought of holding the asset in common and they decide to kill the goose that lays the golden eggs. What then? (The numbers I use are very rough and would vary from place to place, but I'm just trying to make a point.) Let's say they can sell the building for a million dollars. Wow! That's a little over $333,000 each! But wait, there's the cost of the transaction: real estate agents, lawyers, taxes. Let's say at the end of the day each heir is left with $275,000. Nothing to sneeze at right? But where will they each get an investment that provides a return on equity of $33,000 on $275, 000 annually? That would be a return of over twelve percent per annum! They were getting ten percent return before—but that was on a mature investment. They are far more likely to get around five percent, if that. If they can get that, they will have managed to turn $33,000 per annum into $13,750 per annum—or less.

So, what's an alternative? In the olden days there was something called *primogeniture*. Primogeniture allowed you to retain assets whole. The conventional wisdom on primogeniture is the firstborn got everything and the others got nothing. But this misses the intent. The oldest held the estate in trust as the new head of his father's house.

Now you know why the oldest son was favored in so many traditional cultures. Mothers and even grandmothers fawned over him because these women knew intuitively that they may have to rely upon him some day. Naturally siblings resented this, especially younger brothers. But generally the brothers wanted to usurp the oldest, not jettison the custom. When the time came to pass on the headship of their own houses they resorted to the same thing.

The Paterfamilias: Primogeniture and Salvation

In Christianity salvation is through Christ alone. Why is that? It is because he is the only begotten Son of God and the sole heir. After his crucifixion he was raised from the dead and he ascended to heaven. As heir apparent he is seated at the right hand of the Father. At the end of time he will take possession of his inheritance. He gets everything. Those who believe in him are joint heirs because they are connected to him, like a body to its head. This is what it means to be *in Christ*. It is classic primogeniture.

Fighting Fire with Fire

Primogeniture didn't work so well in practice. Just a glance at the folklore of the younger son will tell you that. But even that isn't enough to justify primogeniture's bad name. Egalitarians condemn it prima facie because it is hierarchical. Nonetheless, it may still be the best option if keeping an estate whole is the goal. But the best way to make it work, in effect if not in name, may be with an unlikely legal instrument.

Throughout this book I have pointed out repeatedly that corporations have marginalized households. But unless something very unexpected happens they're here to stay. That being the case, perhaps it is time to join in the fun. It may be time to incorporate our households.

The notion is not as radical as it may sound. The name corporation implies that these entities are not aggregations of individuals, from a legal point of view they are persons. They have interests. They can own property. These things, if you haven't noticed by now, were once considered true of households.

The corporation would need to be flexible and customizable, as well as easy to set up and keep going. It would need to be capable of holding a wide variety of assets and be able to accommodate a wide range of people and interests. Well, it just so happens that we have such a thing. It is called a *Limited Liability Company*, or *LLC* for short. Let's take a look at how it could work for households.

(Before I continue, let me add these caveats: I'm not a lawyer, nor am I a tax accountant. This is merely a thought experiment.)

The purpose of the LLC would be to hold productive property. In an LLC owners are called "Members." The executive is called the "Managing Member." (The work of a Managing Member corresponds nicely to a head of house.) Percentages of ownership would be assigned to members while making sure the managing member retains control. Once the articles of corporation are filed, it can open a bank account, own property, and make distributions to members as it sees fit. Succession could work like primogeniture should have worked. (The plan would have to be included in the articles of incorporation.) In the best case scenario the father would turn over the management of the corporation to the new Managing Member before death. Once the father dies the only matter to be resolved is the distribution of the father's share. The beauty of all this is the court is left with little to do—so long as people remain civil, that is. But best of all, since the household is incorporated, in the event of incivility, the civil authorities can be brought in to adjudicate the dispute—ideally along the lines established by the articles of incorporation.

Another Objection

But what about heirs who want to go their own ways? Yes, ideally there should be ways to let them.

But what should be questioned before they go is their notion of freedom. We are never free in an absolute sense. Freedom is a formula; to be free from one thing, you must depend on something else. Most people today depend on the corporate economy to maintain their freedom from the demands of self-employment and business ownership. But the price of that freedom is wage slavery.

Liberty in the old-fashioned sense means that you depend on things you have some real say about: things like land you own, or a business you own, or even the members of your own household. Maybe we should stop asking our kids, "What do you want to be when you grow up?" Instead we might ask them, "What do you want to depend on the rest of your life?" The first question conceals dependency, the second freedom.

The Paterfamilias: A Biblical Vision of Liberty

Each of them will sit under his vine and under his fig tree, and with no one to make them afraid. For the mouth of the Lord has spoken (Micah 4:4).

What Is the Future of the Household?

So here's my prediction for what it's worth: a barbell is forming. On one side are local economies—functional households among other things—and on the other is a borderless global marketplace. It's the stuff in the middle that is getting thin. As the costs of small-scale production come down, and access to global markets opens up for the little guy, the advantages of economies of scale and proprietary distribution systems go away. Small, nimble producers of highly customized goods are already thriving. This phenomenon, along with new ways to access capital, and the collapse of social insurance, will lead to a revival of relatively small, voluntary mutual aid associations. In such a world the household economy is viable again. It may even be necessary.

Leaving a House for Your Dependents

I am nearing the end of this little handbook and as I do so I am getting closer to your death (both in fact and metaphorically—but mostly the latter). If you want your household to live on after you are gone, not only will you need to think clearly about your death; the people closest to you will need to too. And when you all do that you may find that one or more of the daunting tasks listed below will need to be performed.

Depending on Your Children

If you've ever said, "I don't want to be a burden to my children" then you need to get over yourself. If you live so long, you will be a burden, if not to your children, then to the children of other people. Social Security, socialized medicine, and even your 401K merely shift the burden from people you know to people you don't know. As I've said, when it comes to social insurance, economically productive people pay into it so that the funds can be redistributed to people who are not economically productive. So there you are—still a burden. It is the anonymity of the system that gives you the illusion of independence.

It was this need for support in old age that once justified the moral strictures of the old household: honoring your parents, submitting to (and putting up with) their involvement in your affairs, and so on. But there was an important caveat: aged parents were supposed to provide the very means needed to support them in the end. When your decrepit father comes to live with you, he ought to hand over the business if he hasn't already, and the investment real estate, not to mention the dividend yielding stock. His cost in upkeep shouldn't be too great. Mostly he'll need physical help. If we get back to a household-centered economy the social welfare aspects will come too. Will it be easy? No. Why do you suppose we have nursing homes?

Many of the practices of our ancestors actually had a reasonable basis, and were not, as we like to tell ourselves, the products of senseless convention or superstition. But if there is a practice that strikes us as impossible to justify rationally, it is the next one I will consider.

Arranging Marriage

Much ink has been spilt over how unfair and cruel the custom of arranged marriage was. I am sure that at times it was. But I have actually known some couples in arranged marriages and they seemed happy enough. On the other hand I've also known many unhappily married people who've had no one to blame but themselves for their misery.

I suspect that some form of arranged marriage is inevitable if we do return to a household-centered economy. When you rely on the state, or a pension plan, to care for you in your old age, arranged marriage can't help but seem meddlesome.

The Paterfamilias:
"If I Bend Anymore, I'll Break!"

Tevye, the kind-hearted Jewish patriarch of *Fiddler on the Roof*, is trying to keep his balance in a modernizing world. In the past, tradition had been the foundation, something objective and proven. But the modern world trusts desire, something subjective and beyond the light of moral judgment. Tevye learns that in this new world a father's only job is to bless whatever his child has already decided to do.

When it comes to the romantic interests of his daughters, Tevye does his best to adjust himself to the new arrangement. He consoles himself with the thought that his daughters are happy with their choices. The first daughter falls in love with a poor tailor—a mousy man that Tevye doubts can properly care for her; but he's willing to be proven wrong. His second daughter falls in love with a Communist. Tevye admires the fellow's idealism. But he has misgivings about his heterodox beliefs and he fears that his daughter will be neglected. But when it comes to his third daughter, Tevye reaches his limit. She has fallen in love with a Christian.

There is accommodation, and then there is betrayal. Tevye agonizes, trying to reconcile his love for his daughter with his responsibilities as the head of a Jewish house, but he just can't do it. He finally cries, "If I bend anymore, I'll break!" Then he disowns her. She has chosen to turn her back on her faith and in so doing her father's house. The judgment is hers; Tevye simply confirms it. Blessing the union would be a betrayal of the very terms of the blessing. It would be empty. She is on her own.

So let's get right to the issue. If you have acquired productive property, it cared for you as you cared for it. When you're gone, hopefully it will go on caring for your children and your grandchildren. The people you leave behind will include some people they've married. What about that? Should you just leave it to them and hope for the best? The assertion that who they marry is none of your business is absurd.

Now, this is not a book on arranging marriages. I'm merely raising a point here, a very broad one with a lot of room for interpretation. And that point is merely this: *whom your children marry is your business*. It isn't solely your business, but you deserve a say, for the good of your children, and for your own good.

Disowning a Child

A friend once said to me, "You shouldn't hire someone until you have first had to fire someone." It wasn't bravado. It was a little dose of reality. What he was getting at is this: *If you know what would cause you to fire someone, you know what to screen for before you hire someone.*

We don't get to screen our kids before we have them (and I hope that we never do). The closest we should get to that is screening for a good mate. In the course of a family business, there may come a time when firing a son or a daughter is necessary. But you may need to take it one step further, it may be necessary to cut a child off completely.

You never hear of that today. If anything we see the polar opposite—the mother of the accused appears on television to say, "Johnny is a good boy. He ain't hurt nobody." Then Johnny's mug-shot flashes on screen and you think: *he did it.*

There truly are crimes so repugnant, so treasonous, so inhumane, that failure to disown a child who commits such a crime is a betrayal of the human race. Doing less would be in some sense a further injustice to the victims. If your son were Hitler, would you disown him? I hope so.

We should be very slow to act, leaving plenty of space and time for the child to come to himself. Still, there are children so incorrigible that we know what the outcome will probably be.

In one sense no one *deserves* an inheritance. But justice *must* account for merit. What's fair about equally dividing an estate between a son who has managed to set up his own business, a daughter who has faithfully cared for her aging parents, and another daughter who has dropped out of high school and has had three children out of wedlock by three different men? Wouldn't justice dictate an unequal distribution? Perhaps the fair thing would be to give the son one and a half shares, the first daughter one share, and the remaining daughter nothing, but giving a half share to her children in the form of a trust.

Finally, talent matters. If that bothers you, remember that Jesus had something to say about talent. In the parable of the talents three stewards were entrusted with a portion of a master's estate. One received five talents, another two, and the last, just one. According to the story the most talented steward took his five and gained five more for a total of ten. The second doubled his portion too for a total of four. But the least talented fellow did not get a return at all. He hid his talent. When the stewards reported to the master, the least talented steward's only talent was taken from him and given to the most talented guy. If our feelings were the only consideration we might favor the least talented fellow and condemn Jesus for such a heartless story. But feelings are not the only consideration.

Most of us have a hard time with this because of our affection for our children. This is understandable, but it misses the point. We're not dealing with sentiment; we're dealing with a livelihood here. Our sentiments need to be tempered by wisdom. Sure, we can get things wrong—and our judgments can even be misled by our grievances. But a livelihood is the main thing; and for that you need talent and virtue. Is the child capable? Is he wise? Is he self-controlled? Is he loyal? These are the proper considerations.

> *The Paterfamilias: Becoming a Child of Abraham*
>
> We've come full circle, back to covenants and inheritances.
>
> Our households will die eventually, and everything we pass on to our heirs will fade away in time. But there is one household that will live on forever.
>
> Joseph C. Atkinson in his monumental study, *Biblical and Theological Foundations of the Family*, shows that both Jews and Christians have believed that our families can be carriers of the covenant God made with Abraham
>
> Christians believe that Jesus is both the true child of promise; he is the promised Messiah. His household will never end and the good news is that we can enter his house. Our houses can become a part of his, like Russian nesting dolls.
>
> Your household can even be a witness to the household of God by the way it works. This, if you haven't noticed, is what this book has been all about.

You are a steward of the good things that God has placed in your care. Hopefully you will have prospered by the time you reach the end of your earthly life. Eventually you must entrust your goods to others. It is your last act of stewardship. You must judge; refusing to judge is itself a judgment—by failing to judge you in effect say talent and merit just don't count.

The Conclusion of the Matter

When we can, we should bless our children. But blessings can lie on the surface like snow, or they can seep in and make a life fruitful.

An inheritance can do either. It can contain everything except the essential thing. Sometimes you see this—a child inherits a fortune but not the virtue needed to care for it. Worse, because he has everything but virtue, he may never even feel the need of it. But if the essential thing is received, the child will prosper, even if he receives no possessions to go along with it.

But virtue is the most difficult thing of all to give someone, because it really isn't ours to give. It has to be drawn out of the person himself.

Through the seasons of life your children will watch you, they will hear what you say, and they will feel the impress of your will. But it will all lie on the surface like so much snow unless there is something else. Something needs to happen; warmth must come from below. It isn't science. It isn't even art. It is a work of grace. That is the essential thing.

The most enlightened tyrants handle people tenderly. And their subjects smilingly succumb to their mothering. I am told that those who are dying in the snow feel strangely warm just before they fall asleep for the last time. But the just man, who has sired virtuous children, enjoys watching them warm themselves.

A parting thought: if your household can retain its independence-through moral virtue, like Noah and his house, your heirs may someday step into in a world wiped clean. It is my hope and prayer that this book has encouraged you to build a house that can weather the coming storm.

Afterword

Allan C. Carlson

Nearly 400 years ago, a band of Englishmen resolved to leave their troubled and morally corrupted homeland, to create a new polity across the Atlantic where they might successfully rear children in righteousness and fear of the Lord. Witnessing the early tremors of the urban-industrial revolution, they committed themselves to subsistence agriculture grounded in self-sufficiency. In place of production for sale, they focused on production for use, supplemented by communal sharing. In diversified farm and artisan production and through family labor involving adults and children, they sought security.

Their close-knit villages were, in one historian's words, "small, intimate, and essentially cooperative" places, resting on "good neighborliness," or friendship. Social order grew out an acceptance of authority grounded in covenants freely embraced. Appalled by the drastic inequalities found in England, they implemented an equitable division of productive land. This intentional focus on building and sustaining a "middling class" meant that each man had the "opportunity to live a long life on his own land among a group of equals."

This new commonwealth was intensely family-centered. One early leader explained that there were three kinds of society: the domestic, the ecclesiastical, and the political. In good Aristotelian style, he emphasized that "the domestic is the first instituted and in some ways the most pivotally important." Work was organized along family lines, rather than through a wage system and marketplace. Economic prosperity came through the purposeful labor of successive generations; parents raised their children to succeed them, not to succeed. Early marriage was the expectation, and reality.

Grounded in marriage and purposeful sexuality, the households of these New World colonists were rich in functions and activity. They were the central agencies of both production and exchange. They were the schools where parents educated the children under their care. In addition, they were vocational training centers, churches, hospitals, welfare institutions, retirement homes, and even houses of correction. Above all, these households were centers dedicated to "parental ministry," signs of an entire polity committed first and foremost to the rearing of Godly children.

Holding this whole commonwealth together were fathers conscious of their enormous, vital, and necessary duties. Their responsible dominion imparted strength to those living under their rule. The daily duties of these fathers included leading the household in prayer, reading Holy Scripture, singing hymns, and offering thanks to the Lord at mealtimes. They also would regularly examine the spiritual state of those under their charge. Governments and congregations existed primarily to support fathers in these critical tasks.

Such was the world of the 17th Century Puritans. Mostly ridiculed in our day, these colonists actually built a Christian commonwealth that was remarkably successful: nearly universal marriage among adults; a boisterous fertility, with an average of nine births per family (in one village an average of 11.6!); exceptionally good health when compared to populations in the Old World; and relative peace and harmony. In the words of a pair of historians: "Stable and patriarchal, . . . the New England family guaranteed peace and good order."

C. R. Wiley's *Man of the House* is a worthy and valuable heir to the great tracts on the foundations for a good life in this world as penned by the Puritan worthies, by reformers such as Martin Luther, by the Church Fathers of the early Christian centuries, and even by the Greek philosophers. Wiley properly states that this is not a history book, but rather a plan for contemporary action. In a deeper sense, though, this deceptively simple volume reaches creatively into the past to find and clarify ways for Christian families to survive—and even thrive—in a world that is falling apart.

Challenging accepted economic wisdom (while simultaneously agreeing with both Aristotle and Cotton Mather), Wiley combines idealism and common sense in his call for recreation of active, productive, meaningful households as the most promising means of social reconstruction. Agreeing with Luther, Wiley emphasizes the absolutely necessary role of "housefathers" (or husbands) in this task. His lively discussions of the value of child labor and of wives as a source of wealth are equally "politically incorrect," yet profoundly insightful and important guides toward a better future.

I joyfully commend this book to Christian men and women as a guide toward building a new family-centered polity in a troubled age, as a light for a new generation of God-fearing "colonists" in the 21st Century.

Allan C. Carlson is President Emeritus of The Howard Center for Family, Religion & Society, founder of The World Congress of Families, editor of The Natural Family: An International Journal of Research and Policy, and the author of fourteen books, including most recently Family Cycles: Strength, Decline & Renewal in Domestic Life, 1630–2000.

Suggestions for Further Reading

SOME OF THE IDEAS presented in Man of the House may be new to you. If you're the sort of person who likes to get to the roots of things, this list of suggested books may prove helpful.

Adorno, Theodor W., and Frenkel-Brunswik, Else. *The Authoritarian Personality.* New York: W. W. Norton, 1993.

Aesop. *Aesop's Fables.* Translated by Laura Gibbs. New York: Oxford University Press, 2008.

Aristotle. *Aristotle's Nichomachean Ethics.* Translated by Robert C. Bartlett and Susan D. Collins. Chicago: The University of Chicago Press, 2011.

———. *Aristotle's Politics: Second Edition.* Translated by Carnes Lords. Chicago: The University of Chicago Press, 2013.

Atkinson, Joseph C. *Biblical and Theological Foundations of the Family: The Domestic Church.* Washington, D.C.: The Catholic University Press of America, 2014.

Berry, Wendell. *Life Is a Miracle: An Essay Against Modern Superstition.* Berkeley: Counterpoint, 2000.

———. *The Way of Ignorance: And Other Essays.* Berkeley: Counterpoint, 2005.

———. *What Are People For?* New York: North Point, 1990.

Boersma, Hans. *Heavenly Participation: The Weaving of a Sacramental Tapestry.* Grand Rapids: Eerdmans, 2011.

Brague, Remi. The Wisdom of the World: The Human Experience of the Universe in Western Thought. Translated by Teresa Lavender Fagan. Chicago: The University of Chicago Press, 2003.

Carlson, Allan C. The Family in America: Searching for Social Harmony in the Industrial Age. New Brunswick: Transaction, 2007.

———. Third Ways: How Bulgarian Greens, Swedish Housewives, and Beer-Swilling Englishmen Created Family-Centered Economies—and Why They Disappeared. Wilmington: ISI, 2007.

Crawford, Matthew B. Shop Class as Soulcraft: An Inquiry into the Value of Work. New York: Penguin, 2009.

Dupre, Louis. Passage to Modernity: An Essay in the Hermeneutics of Nature and Culture. New Haven: Yale University Press, 1993.

Eberstadt, Mary. How the West Really Lost God: A New Theory of Secularization. West Conshohocken: Templeton, 2013.

Ellickson, Robert C. The Household: Informal Order Around the Hearth. Princeton: Princeton University Press, 2008.

Hansen, Marcus Lee. The Problem of the Third Generation Immigrant,

Heinlein, Robert. Time Enough for Love. New York: Ace, 1988.

Horowitz, Sara. "America, say goodbye to the Era of Big Work." Los Angles Times (August 25, 2014)

Huxley, Aldous. Brave New World. New York: Harper Perennial Modern Classics, 2006

James, P. D. The Children of Men. New York: Vintage, 2006.

Jauhar, Sandeep. "Why Doctors Are Sick of Their Profession." Wall Street Journal (August 29, 2014) C,1–2.

Junger, Sebastian. Tribe: On Homecoming and Belonging. New York: Twelve, 2016.

Kline, Meredith G. Kingdom Prologue: Genesis Foundations for a Covenantal Worldview. Eugene: Wipf and Stock, 2006.

Kornrich, Sabino, Julie Brines, and Katrina Leupp "Egalitarianism, Housework, and Sexual Frequency in Marriage." American Sociological Review 78 (2012) 26–50.

Lasch, Christopher. Haven in a Heartless World: The Family Besieged. New York: W. W. Norton, 1977.

Lewis, C. S. The Abolition of Man. New York: HarperOne, 2001.

———. The Discarded Image. New York: Cambridge University Press, 2012.

———. Surprised by Joy: The Shape of My Early Life. Orlando: Harcourt, Brace, Jovanovich, 1966.

Locke, John. The Second Treatise of Government and A Letter Concerning Toleration. New York: Dover, 2002

MacIntyre, Alasdair. After Virtue. Notre Dame: University of Notre Dame Press, 1984.

Nisbet, Robert. The Quest for Community: A Study in the Ethics of Order and Freedom. Wilmington: ISI, 1990.

Pieper, Josef. Leisure: The Basis of Culture. San Francisco: Ignatius, 2009.

Plato. Plato's Symposium: A Translation by Seth Berardete with Commentary by Allan Bloom and Seth Berardete. Chicago: The University of Chicago Press, 2001.

———. The Republic. Translated by R. E. Allen. New Haven: Yale University Press, 2006.

Podles, Leon J. The Church Impotent: The Feminization of Christianity. Dallas: Spence, 1999.

Schumacher, E. F. Small Is Beautiful: Economics as if People Mattered. New York: HarperPerennial, 1989

Stanley, Thomas J. and Danko, William D. The Millionaire Next Door: The Surprising Secrets of America's Wealthy. Lanham: Taylor Trade, 2010.

Tolkien, J. R. R. The Lord of the Rings: 50th Anniversary One Volume Edition. Great Britain: HarperCollins, 2004

Weaver, Richard M. Ideas Have Consequences. Chicago: The University of Chicago Press, 1984.

Woodruff, Paul. The Ajax Dilemma: Justice, Fairness, and Rewards. New York: Oxford University Press, 2011.

———. Reverence: Renewing a Forgotten Virtue. New York: Oxford University Press, 2014.

88845505R00090

Made in the USA
Lexington, KY
18 May 2018